FUTURE
English for Results

INTRO

WORKBOOK with AUDIO CD

Jennifer Asp

Kate Mueller

Series Consultants

Beatriz B. Díaz

Ronna Magy

Federico Salas-Isnardi

PEARSON
Longman

Future Intro
English for Results
Workbook with Audio CD

Pearson Education, 10 Bank Street, White Plains, NY 10606

Staff credits: The people who made up the *Future Intro Workbook* team, representing editorial, production, design, and manufacturing, are Jennifer Adamec, Elizabeth Carlson, Aerin Csigay, Dave Dickey, Nancy Flaggman, Irene Frankel, Shelley Gazes, Michael Kemper, Liza Pleva, and Barbara Sabella.

Cover design: Rhea Banker
Cover photo: Kathy Lamm/Getty Images
Text design: Barbara Sabella
Text composition: Rainbow Graphics
Text font: 12 pt Helvetica Neue

Illustration credits: Steve Attoe: pp. 15, 23, 28, 92 (bottom), 100, 125 (bottom), 135; Kenneth Batelman: p. 74; Luis Briseno: pp. 13 (bottom), 80; Laurie Conley: pp. 18-19, 42, 75 (bottom), 77, 92 (top), 105, 139, 124, 128, 138, 139, 140; Deborah Crowle: p. 2; Len Ebert: pp. 39, 115; Scott Fray: pp. 25, 26, 27, 70 (bottom), 87; Peter Grau: pp. 12, 24, 36, 48, 60, 72, 84, 96, 108, 120, 132, 144; Brian Hughes: pp. 10, 54, 57, 68, 69, 70 (top), 75 (top), 84, 111, 113, 117, 130, 131; Stephen Hutchings: pp. 16, 89, 125 (top); Paul McCusker: pp. 90, 91, 99, 123, 129; Chris Murphy: pp. 44, 46; Roberto Sadi: pp. 35, 116 ; Neil Stewart/NSV Productions: p. 59; Meryl Treatner: p. 43; Anna Veltfort: pp. 88, 93, 104, 114, 126, 127

Photo credits: All original photography by David Mager. Page 3(2) Pablo Delfos/agefotostock; 4(bottom) Blend Images/Jupiterimages; 5 Shutterstock; 8 Shutterstock; 9(2) Shutterstock, (4) Shutterstock, (5) Jupiterimages/Creatas/Alamy, (8) Shutterstock; 11 Corbis/Jupiterimages; 14(a) Shutterstock, (b) Stockbyte/Getty Images, (d) Shutterstock, (e) Dreamstime.com, (f) Shutterstock, (g) Shutterstock, (h) Michael Newman/PhotoEdit, (i) Shutterstock; 37 Corbis/Jupiterimages; 38(1) Shutterstock, (4) Shutterstock, (5) iStockphoto.com, (7) Shutterstock, (8) Shutterstock, (9) Shutterstock; 40 Jose Luis Pelaez Inc/Jupiterimages; 49 Photos.com/Jupiterimages; 52(1) M Stock/Alamy, (2) David Young-Wolff/PhotoEdit, (3) Lushpix/age fotostock, (4) Shutterstock, (5) Shutterstock, (6) Bill Aron/PhotoEdit; 55 Bob Daemmrich/PhotoEdit; 61 Glowimages/Getty Images; 62(1) iStockphoto.com, (2) Shutterstock, (3) Shutterstock, (4) Shutterstock, (5) Shutterstock, (6) Shutterstock, (7) Shutterstock, (8) Shutterstock, (9) Shutterstock; 63 Shutterstock; 66 Shutterstock; 71(a) Shutterstock, (b) Dana Hoff/Beateworks/Corbis, (c) iStockphoto.com, (d) Shutterstock, (e) Shutterstock, (f) Shutterstock; 73 Shutterstock; 76(a) Shutterstock, (b) Red Cover/Getty Images, (c) Peter Durant/Arcaid/Corbis, (d) Bigstockphoto.com; 77 Shutterstock; 78(1) Michael Newman/PhotoEdit, (2) iStockphoto.com, (3) Shutterstock, (4) Echos/Jupiterimages, (5) Jupiterimages/Comstock Images/Alamy, (6) Shutterstock, (7) C Squared Studios/Getty Images, (8) David Toase/Getty Images, (9) Bigstockphoto.com, (10) Photos.com/Jupiterimages, (11) Shutterstock, (12) Shutterstock; 86(1) Shutterstock, (2) David Young-Wolff/PhotoEdit, (3) Photos.com/Jupiterimages, (4) Shutterstock, (5) Shutterstock, (7) Canstockphoto.com, (9) Shutterstock, (10) Dorling Kindersley, (11) iStockphoto.com, (12) iStockphoto.com; 91 Shutterstock; 94(BL) Photos.com/Jupiterimages; 95 Shutterstock; 98(a) Shutterstock, (b) Dreamstime.com, (c) Malcolm Case-Green/Alamy, (d) Sami Sarkis Lifestyles/Alamy, (e) Diane Macdonald/Getty Images, (f) iStockphoto.com, (g) Shutterstock, (h) Donald Miralle/Getty Images, (i) Michael Newman/PhotoEdit; 102(1) Index Stock Imagery, (2) RubberBall/Alamy, (3) Shutterstock, (4) Colin Young-Wolff/PhotoEdit, (5) Jupiterimages/Comstock Images/Alamy, (6) Kayte M. Deioma/PhotoEdit, (7) I love images/Jupiterimages; (8) iStockphoto.com, (9) David J. Green - Lifestyle/Alamy; 110(a) Rob Crandall/The Image Works, (b) Jeff Greenberg/The Image Works, (c) Photodisc/Getty Images, (d) Jeff Greenberg/PhotoEdit; (e) Will & Deni McIntyre/Photo Researchers, Inc., (f) Tom Carter/PhotoEdit, (g) MedioImages/age fotostock, (h) David R. Frazier/PhotoEdit, (i) Shutterstock; 112(1) Tom Prettyman/PhotoEdit, (2) Cathy Datwani, (3) Cathy Datwani, (4) Jeff Greenberg/PhotoEdit, (5) David R. Frazier/PhotoEdit, (6) Peter Bennett/Ambient, (7) David R. Frazier/PhotoEdit, (8) Pixtal/SuperStock, (9) Andre Jenny/Alamy; 118(1) Steve Hamblin/Alamy, (2) Shutterstock, (3) Shutterstock, (4) Shutterstock, (5) Shutterstock, (6) Shutterstock, (7) Shutterstock, (8) Shutterstock, (9) Shutterstock; 121(1) Shutterstock, (3) Shutterstock; 133(T) Shutterstock, (B) Shutterstock; 134(a) Shutterstock, (b) MedioImages/Getty Images, (c) Jeff Greenberg/PhotoEdit, (d) Jeff Greenberg/PhotoEdit, (e) Shutterstock, (f) Banana Stock/age fotostock, (g) Frank Herholdt/Getty Images, (h) Kayte M. Deioma/PhotoEdit, (i) David De Lossy/Getty Images; 136(1) Michael Newman/PhotoEdit, (2) Dynamic Graphics/Jupiterimages, (3) iStockphoto.com, (4) Index Stock Imagery, (5) Shutterstock, (6) Shutterstock, (7) Dennis MacDonald/PhotoEdit, (8) Jeff Greenberg/PhotoEdit, (9) Dreamstime.com; 145(2) Shutterstock.

ISBN-13: 978-0-13-240926-1
ISBN-10: 0-13-240926-7

Printed in the United States of America
1 2 3 4 5 6 7 8 9 10—CRS—14 13 12 11 10 09

Contents

To the Teacher

The *Future Intro Workbook with Audio CD* has 12-page units to complement what students have learned in the Student Book. Each Workbook unit follows the lesson order of the Student Book and provides supplemental practice in vocabulary, grammar, listening, life skills, reading, writing, and phonics. Students can complete the exercises outside the classroom as homework or during class time to extend instruction.

The Workbook Audio CD is a unique feature of the Workbook. It provides practice with conversations, vocabulary, grammar, reading, and life skills competencies.

UNIT STRUCTURE

Vocabulary
Each Workbook unit begins with vocabulary practice. There are usually three vocabulary lessons per unit that provide reinforcement activities for the vocabulary lessons in the Student Book. In addition, some of the Life Skills lessons contain relevant vocabulary practice.

Grammar
Grammar is practiced in contextualized exercises that include sentence completion, sentence writing, fill-in, matching, and multiple choice. Grammar exercises also reinforce the new vocabulary taught in that lesson. Some lessons include personalized activities.

Listening
Listening activities in the Workbook are used to complement various skills, including vocabulary, grammar, life skills, reading, and phonics. Activities include listening comprehension, listening dictation, listening and reading, and listening to check answers.

Life Skills
Life Skills lessons provide students with real-life practice. Realia-based exercises are usually featured on these pages. Students complete forms and other realia based on information provided or with personal information. Other activity types include fill-in, matching, and multiple choice.

Writing
Writing is practiced in controlled and personalized activities throughout the Workbook. In each lesson students write words, phrases, and/or sentences.

Reading
The reading page extends the practice provided in the reading lesson in the Student Book. The story featured in the Student Book is presented again, but with the sentences scrambled. Students listen to the audio and number the sentences in the correct order. Then students write the story in the correct order.

Phonics
The Workbook provides additional phonics practice, giving students another opportunity to make connections between the sounds of English and the letters that represent them. Activities include listening dictation, completing words, and listening to check answers.

ADDITIONAL RESOURCES

At the back of the Workbook, you will find:
- Audio Script
- Answer Key
- CD Track list
- Bound-in Audio CD

ORIENTATION

The Workbook, like the Student Book, includes an orientation for students. Before the students use the Workbook for the first time, direct them to To the Student on the next page. Go through the questions and tips with the students and answer any questions they may have so they can get the most out of using the Workbook.

To the Student

LEARN ABOUT YOUR BOOK

A PAIRS. Look in the back of your book. Find each section. Write the page number.

Audio Script ___   Answer Key ___   CD Track list ___

B PAIRS. Look at page 157. Find *Answers will vary.* What does *Answers will vary* mean?

C CLASS. Where is the CD?

D CLASS. Look at page 4. What does ⊙ mean? What does *Play Track 2* mean?

TIPS FOR USING THE AUDIO CD

CLASS. Read the tips for using the audio CD.
- For all exercises, listen to each track many times.
- For dictation exercises, use the pause button ❚❚ so you can have more time to write.
- After you finish the unit, for more listening practice, play the CD again and read the audio script in the back of the book at the same time.
- Also, for more listening practice, listen to the CD when you are in the car or on the bus.

WRITING TIPS

CLASS. Read the writing tips.
- Start sentences with a capital letter.
- End statements with a period. (.)
- End questions with a question mark. (?)

For example:

   My name is Jack.

   What's your name?

Lesson 1: Countries

A Look at the map. Write the countries. Use the countries in the box.

> Cambodia   El Salvador   Mexico   Somalia
> ~~Canada~~   Haiti   Peru   the United States
> China   Korea   Russia   Vietnam

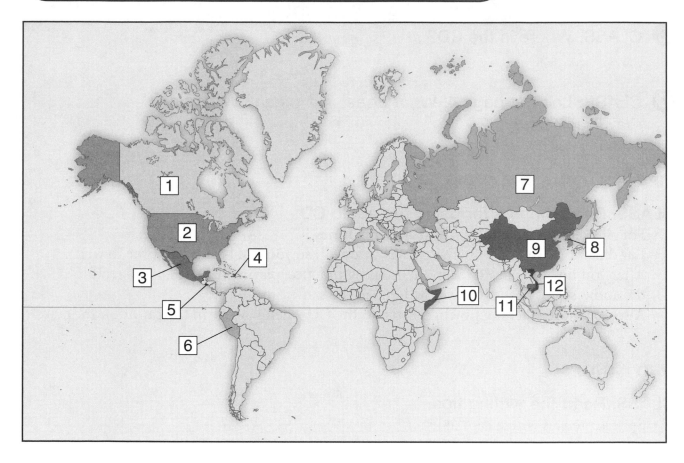

1. _Canada_
2. _____
3. _____
4. _____

5. _____
6. _____
7. _____
8. _____

9. _____
10. _____
11. _____
12. _____

B Look at the pictures. Write the names and the countries.

1.
Maria
El Salvador

    A: What's your name?

    B: My name is _____Maria_____.

    A: Where are you from?

    B: I'm from _____El Salvador_____.

2.
Rosa
Haiti

    A: What's your name?

    B: My name is _____.

    A: Where are you from?

    B: I'm from _____.

3.
Teng
China

    A: What's your name?

    B: My name is _____.

    A: Where are you from?

    B: I'm from _____.

C Write your name and country.

A: What's your name?

B: My name is _____.

A: Where are you from?

B: I'm from _____.

A Write the capital letters of the alphabet.

A B _C_ D E ___ G ___ I ___ ___ L

M N O ___ ___ R ___ T U ___ W ___ ___ Z

B Write the lowercase letters of the alphabet.

a _b_ c ___ e f g h ___ j k ___ ___

n ___ p q ___ s ___ u v ___ x y ___

C 💿 Play Track 2. Listen. Write the names.

1. First name: _H_ _o_ _n_ _g_
   Last name: _C_ _h_ _e_ _n_

2. First name: ___ ___ ___ ___
   Last name: ___ ___ ___ ___ ___

3. First name: ___ ___ ___ ___
   Last name: ___ ___ ___ ___ ___

4. First name: ___ ___ ___ ___ ___
   Last name: ___ ___ ___ ___

A Read the words. Write the numbers. Use the numbers in the box.

| 0 | 1 | 2 | ~~3~~ | 4 | 5 | 6 | 7 | 8 | 9 |

1. three _3_
2. one ____
3. eight ____
4. six ____
5. four ____

6. nine ____
7. five ____
8. zero ____
9. seven ____
10. two ____

B Play Track 3. Listen. Write the student ID numbers.

1. _5_ _3_ _6_ _9_ _1_

2. ___ ___ ___ ___ ___

3. ___ ___ ___ ___ ___

4. ___ ___ ___ ___ ___

STUDENT

Name: **Pavlina Ivanova**

ID Number: **53691**

IDENTIFICATION CARD

C Play Track 4. Listen. Write the telephone numbers.

1. _6_ _7_ _4_ - _5_ _5_ _5_ - _5_ _8_ _3_ _1_

2. ___ ___ ___ - _5_ _5_ _5_ - ___ ___ ___ ___

3. ___ ___ ___ - _5_ _5_ _5_ - ___ ___ ___ ___

4. ___ ___ ___ - _5_ _5_ _5_ - ___ ___ ___ ___

5. ___ ___ ___ - _5_ _5_ _5_ - ___ ___ ___ ___

6. ___ ___ ___ - _5_ _5_ _5_ - ___ ___ ___ ___

A Write *am* or *are*.

1. I _am_ David Green.

2. You _____ a good teacher.

3. You _____ from Peru.

4. I _____ in the classroom.

5. You _____ a good student.

6. I _____ your English teacher.

7. You _____ my classmate.

8. I _____ from China.

B Write *I* or *You*.

1. _You_ are Vue Moua.

2. _____ am from Haiti.

3. _____ am a new student.

4. _____ are the teacher.

5. _____ am from the United States.

6. _____ are a student.

7. _____ are in the library.

8. _____ am your classmate.

C Rewrite the sentences in Exercise B. Use contractions.

1. You're Vue Moua.

2. _____

3. _____

4. _____

5. _____

6. _____

7. _____

8. _____

Ⓐ Look at the pictures. Write *He* or *She.*

1.    _She_ is from Haiti.

2.    _____ is from Poland.

3.    _____ is from Somalia.

4.    _____ is from Canada.

Ⓑ Match the same sentences.

1. She is from China. _b_

2. He is a student. ____

3. He is from Mexico. ____

4. She is in the classroom. ____

a. She's in the classroom.

b. She's from China.

c. He's a student.

d. He's from Mexico.

C 💿 Play Track 5. Listen for *She's* or *He's*. Circle *a* or *b.*

1. (a.) She's b. He's   5. a. She's b. He's
2. a. She's b. He's   6. a. She's b. He's
3. a. She's b. He's   7. a. She's b. He's
4. a. She's b. He's   8. a. She's b. He's

D Write three sentences for each picture. Use *He, She, He's,* or *She's.*

1. Mary / my classmate   *Mary is my classmate.*
   She is my classmate.
   She's my classmate.

2. Mr. Smith / from Canada

3. Ho-Jin / my friend

4. Ms. Rivera / a good teacher

5. Barbara / from Poland

Ⓐ Write *is* or *are.*

1. He __*is*__ a teacher.

2. They _____ my classmates.

3. She _____ from China.

4. They _____ from the United States.

5. Jan and Tom _____ teachers.

6. Michael _____ a student.

7. Annette _____ from Haiti.

8. Eric and Tania _____ good students.

B 🔘 Play Track 6. Listen for *They're, We're,* and *You're.*
Circle *a, b,* or *c.*

1. (a.) They're   b. We're   c. You're

2. a. They're   b. We're   c. You're

3. a. They're   b. We're   c. You're

4. a. They're   b. We're   c. You're

5. a. They're   b. We're   c. You're

6. a. They're   b. We're   c. You're

C Write sentences. Use *You're, We're,* or *They're.*

1. Mai and Tuan are from Vietnam. *They're from Vietnam.*

2. Carlos and I are new students. _____

3. You and Marta are my friends. _____

4. Rafal and Dora are classmates. _____

5. You and Mr. Santos are good teachers. _____

6. Barbara and I are from Poland. _____

7. Ms. Li and Mr. Green are friends. _____

8. You and Carlos are good students. _____

9. Sara and I are friends. _____

10. Ivan and Olga are from Russia. _____

11. Mike and I are in the library. _____

12. You and Ana are classmates. _____

A Read the sentences.

1. My first name is Marie.
2. My middle name is Anne.
3. My last name is Miller.
4. I'm from Canada.
5. My area code is 214.
6. My phone number is 555-5301.
7. My student ID number is 67920.

B Read the sentences again. Fill out the form.

Adult Education Center

Marie

First Name	Middle Name	Last Name

Telephone [   ] – [   ]   **Place of Birth** [   ]

Area Code   Phone Number   Country

Student Identification Number [   ]

A 🖸 Play Track 7. Listen to the story.
Number the sentences in the correct order.

_____ Other students say hello and kiss.

_____ How do you say hello?

_1_ My name is Ivan. I'm a student.

_____ Some students say hello and hug.

_____ I say hello to a classmate and I smile.

_____ Some students say hello and bow.

_____ In my school, some students say hello and shake hands.

B Read the sentences in Exercise A again.
Write the sentences in the correct order.

1. My name is Ivan. I'm a student.

2. _____

3. _____

4. _____

5. _____

6. _____

7. _____

C 🖸 Play Track 7 again to check your answers to Exercise B.

A 🔘 Play Track 8. Listen. Write *m* or *n*.

1. _m_ ap

2. pho____e

3. ____y

4. Chi____a

5. ____exico

6. ____umber

7. classroo____

8. stude____ts

9. ____ice

10. fro____

11. liste____

12. ____eet

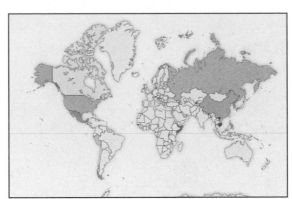

B 🔘 Play Track 9. Listen. Write the words.

1. _____map_____   6. _____

2. _____   7. _____

3. _____   8. _____

4. _____   9. _____

5. _____   10. _____

Lesson 1: Classroom objects

A Match the pictures with the words.

a.

b.

c.

d.

e.

f.

g.

h.

i.

1. a notebook <u>b</u>

2. a book ____

3. a pencil ____

4. a dictionary ____

5. a piece of paper ____

6. an eraser ____

7. a pen ____

8. a cell phone ____

9. a backpack ____

B  Play Track 10. Listen. Choose the correct picture. Circle *a* or *b.*

1. a.   (b.)

2. a.    b.

3. a.   b.

4. a.   b.

5. a. 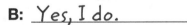   b.

C Look at the picture. Read the questions. Write *Yes, I do* or *No, I don't.*

1. **A:** Do you have a pencil?

   B: _Yes, I do._

2. **A:** Do you have a dictionary?

   B: _____

3. **A:** Do you have a pen?

   B: _____

4. **A:** Do you have a notebook?

   B: _____

5. **A:** Do you have an eraser?

   B: _____

A Look at the pictures. Complete the instructions. Use the words in the box.

Close	Put away	Turn off
Open	Take out	~~Turn on~~

1. _____Turn on_____ your cell phone.

2. _____ your dictionary.

3. _____ the light.

4. _____ your notebook.

5. _____ your book.

6. _____ the door.

B Read the test directions.

TEST DIRECTIONS

1. Put away your books. Don't use a dictionary.

2. Use a pencil. Don't use a pen.

3. Turn off your cell phone.

C Read the test directions again. Circle *Yes* or *No*.

1.	Put away your books.	(Yes)	No
2.	Use a dictionary.	Yes	No
3.	Use a pencil.	Yes	No
4.	Use a pen.	Yes	No
5.	Turn off your cell phone.	Yes	No

D Write negative sentences.

1. Close your book.   *Don't close your book.* _____

2. Use a pencil.   _____

3. Turn on the light.   _____

4. Take out your notebook.   _____

5. Open the door.   _____

6. Put away your dictionary. _____

A Look at the pictures. Complete the words.

1. c_l_as_s_ro_o_m

2. w____m____n's ro____m

3. c____mput____r ____ab

4. ____ff____ce

5. b____oks____or____

6. t____s____ing roo____

7. l____b____ary

8. m____n's r____o____

9. ____af____teri____

Play Track 11. Listen. Choose the correct picture. Circle *a* or *b*.

1. (a.)    b.

2. a.    b.

3. a.    b.

4. a.    b.

5. a.    b.

6. a.    b.

A Look at the map. Write *next to* or *across from*.

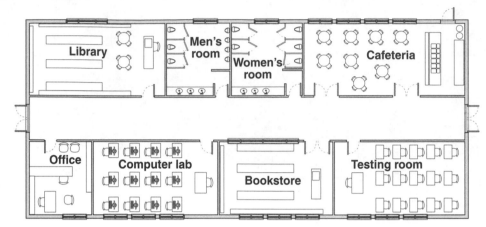

1. Where is the library?

   It's ___*next to*___ the men's room.

2. Where is the bookstore?

   It's _____ the women's room.

3. Where is the testing room?

   It's _____ the cafeteria.

4. Where is the men's room?

   It's _____ the computer lab.

5. Where is the women's room?

   It's _____ the cafeteria.

6. Where is the computer lab?

   It's _____ the office.

B Write sentences about the places in your school. Use *next to* or *across from*. Use the sentence below as a model.

(computer lab) *The computer lab is across from the office.* _____

1. (library) _____

2. (women's room) _____

3. (office) _____

4. (cafeteria) _____

5. (men's room) _____

A Read the form.

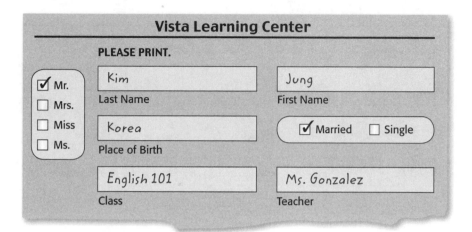

Vista Learning Center

PLEASE PRINT.

☑ Mr.
☐ Mrs.
☐ Miss
☐ Ms.

Kim
Last Name

Jung
First Name

Korea
Place of Birth

☑ Married ☐ Single

English 101
Class

Ms. Gonzalez
Teacher

B Read the form again. Circle *Yes* or *No*.

1. Jung is from Korea.   (Yes)   No

2. Jung is single.   Yes   No

3. Jung is a woman.   Yes   No

4. Jung is in English 102.   Yes   No

5. Ms. Gonzalez is a woman.   Yes   No

6. Ms. Gonzalez is Jung's teacher.   Yes   No

C Fill out the form. Use true or made-up information.

Student Information Form

V ista
L earning
C enter

☐ Mr.   ☐ Mrs.   ☐ Miss   ☐ Ms.

Name _____
       First   Last

Class _____ Teacher _____

Place of Birth _____ Female ☐   Male ☐

A Match the pictures with the words.

a.

b.

c.

d.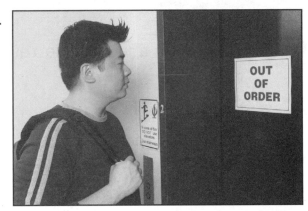

e.

f.

1. use a dictionary __c__

2. read signs ____

3. write in my notebook ____

4. go to class ____

5. practice with my classmates ____

6. ask the teacher questions ____

B 🖸 Play Track 12. Listen. Write the missing words.

A: How do you study English?

B: I ____go____ to class, and I _____ the teacher questions.

A: That's great!

B: How do you study English?

A: I _____ with my classmates. At home, I _____ in my notebook.

C Circle the correct verbs.

1. I (use) / **write** a dictionary.

2. I **go** / **read** signs.

3. I **study** / **go** English at school.

4. I **practice** / **talk** to people.

5. I **write** / **ask** new words.

6. I **ask** / **practice** the teacher questions.

7. I **go** / **use** to the library.

8. I **study** / **write** in my notebook.

9. I **practice** / **use** with my classmates.

10. I **talk** / **go** to class.

D How do *you* study English? Write your answer.
Use the sentence below as a model.

I go to class and I use a dictionary. _____

_____

_____

Ⓐ 💿 **Play Track 13. Listen to the story.
Number the sentences in the correct order.**

____ In my country, students don't talk in class.

____ In the United States, students talk in groups.

____ My teacher listens to the students.

_1_ My name is Lan.

____ They listen to the teacher.

____ In my class, students ask many questions.

Ⓑ **Read the sentences in Exercise A again.
Write the sentences in the correct order.**

1. _My name is Lan._

2. _____

3. _____

4. _____

5. _____

6. _____

Ⓒ 💿 **Play Track 13 again to check your answers to Exercise B.**

A Look at the pictures. Write *p* or *b*.

1. __p__en

2. note____ook

3. ____encil

4. ____ook

5. ____iece of ____a____er

6. ____ack____ack

B Play Track 14 to check your answers to Exercise A.

C Play Track 15. Listen. Write the words.

1. _____pen_____

6. _____

2. _____

7. _____

3. _____

8. _____

4. _____

9. _____

5. _____

10. _____

A 🔘 Play Track 16. Listen for the number. Circle *a* or *b*.

1. a. 7   (b.) 9

2. a. 18   b. 15

3. a. 23   b. 28

4. a. 36   b. 35

5. a. 44   b. 40

6. a. 52   b. 57

B Match the times with the clocks.

a.

b.

c.

d.

e.

f.

1. 6:10 __b__   3. 2:15 ____   5. 1:50 ____

2. 11:05 ____   4. 4:00 ____   6. 8:30 ____

C Look at each clock. Write the time.

1. ___8:10___

2. _____

3. _____

4. _____

5. _____

6. _____

A Complete the sentences. Use the words in the box.

> at   from   time   ~~What~~

1. **A:** __What__ time is your English class?

   B: It's _____ 1:00 to 5:00.

   A: What _____ is your break?

   B: It's _____ 2:15.

> at   is   time   to

2. **A:** What _____ is your English class?

   B: It's from 6:00 _____ 9:00.

   A: What time _____ your break?

   B: It's _____ 7:45.

B Play Track 17. Listen for the time. Circle *a* or *b*.

1. (a.) 9:15   b. 9:50

2. a. 10:14   b. 10:40

3. a. 12:13   b. 12:30

4. a. 2:45   b. 2:40

C Play Track 18. Listen. Write the times you hear.

1. It's from __9:15__ to __1:15__.

2. It's from _____ to _____.

3. It's from _____ to _____.

4. It's from _____ to _____.

D Look at the chart. Circle *Yes* or *No*.

Place	From	To
Cafeteria	11:00 A.M.	1:30 P.M.
School	7:00 A.M.	7:00 P.M.
Computer lab	10:15 A.M.	3:45 P.M.
Office	7:30 A.M.	4:30 P.M.
Library	11:00 A.M.	5:30 P.M.
Bookstore	9:15 A.M.	12:00 P.M.

1. The cafeteria is open at 11:00 A.M.   (Yes)   No

2. The school is open from 7:00 A.M. to 8:30 P.M.   Yes   No

3. The computer lab is open at 10:00 A.M.   Yes   No

4. The office is open from 7:00 A.M. to 4:30 P.M.   Yes   No

5. The library is open at 3:30 P.M.   Yes   No

6. The bookstore is open from 9:15 A.M. to 12:00 P.M.   Yes   No

E Write sentences. Use *from/to* or *at*.

1. The library is open / 9:00 *The library is open at 9:00.*

2. My break is / 2:00 / 2:20 _____

3. The cafeteria is open / 7:00 / 3:00 _____

4. My computer class starts / 4:30 _____

5. The office is open / 11:30 _____

6. My English class is / 10:00 / 12:00 _____

7. The computer lab is open / 8:00 / 11:00 _____

8. My break is over / 3:00 _____

A Match the pictures with the words.

a.

b.

c.

d.

e.

f.

g.

h.

i.

1. go to sleep __c__

2. get up ____

3. eat breakfast ____

4. take a shower ____

5. eat lunch ____

6. get dressed ____

7. go to school ____

8. go to work ____

9. get home ____

B Write about yourself. Use true or made-up information. Use the sentence below as a model.

get up   _I get up at 7:00 A.M._

1. take a shower   _____

2. get dressed   _____

3. eat breakfast   _____

4. go to work   _____

5. go to school   _____

6. get home   _____

C Write the correct form of the verb.

1. Clara (go) _____ _goes_ _____ to sleep at 9:00.

2. Ho-Jin (take) _____ a shower at 6:30.

3. Alicia (get) _____ dressed at 8:00.

4. Julian (eat) _____ lunch at 12:30.

5. Mia (get up) _____ at 7:00.

6. Victor (go) _____ to work at 8:30.

D Play Track 19. Listen for the daily activity. Circle *a* or *b.*

1. (a.) goes to work   b. takes a shower

2. a. eats lunch   b. gets dressed

3. a. goes to sleep   b. goes to school

4. a. eats breakfast   b. eats lunch

5. a. gets up   b. gets home

A Complete the schedule. Write the days in the box in the correct order.

> Friday   Monday   Saturday   ~~Sunday~~   Thursday   Tuesday   Wednesday

Sunday	_____	_____	_____	_____	_____	_____
	Work 8–4	Class 11–3	Work 8–4	Class 11–3	Work 8–4	Work 10–2

B Play Track 20. Listen for the day. Circle *a* or *b*.

1. (a.) Monday   b. Wednesday
2. a. Friday   b. Wednesday
3. a. Sunday   b. Saturday
4. a. Tuesday   b. Thursday
5. a. Saturday   b. Sunday

C Complete the sentences. Write *from/to* and *on*.

1. Paul works _from_ Monday _to_ Thursday.

2. Sun-Li goes to school _____ Friday.

3. Robert goes to the library _____ Saturday.

4. Elaine studies English _____ 8:00 _____ 11:00 in the morning.

5. Ivan gets home late _____ Tuesday.

6. Kamila gets up at 6:30 _____ Tuesday _____ Friday.

D Read Mark's schedule.

Schedule

Sunday
Soccer   12:00–3:00

Monday
Work   9:00–2:00

Tuesday
English class   11:00–3:00

Wednesday
Work   9:00–2:00

Thursday
Library   4:00–7:00

Friday
Work   8:00–12:00

Saturday
Soccer   12:00–3:00

E Read Mark's schedule again. Circle *Yes* or *No*.

1.	Mark plays soccer two days a week.	(Yes)	No
2.	He goes to work three days a week.	Yes	No
3.	He goes to work from 8:00 to 12:00 on Monday.	Yes	No
4.	His English class starts at 3:00.	Yes	No
5.	Mark goes to English class two days a week.	Yes	No
6.	He goes to the library on Thursday.	Yes	No
7.	He plays soccer on Friday.	Yes	No
8.	He plays soccer on Saturday.	Yes	No

Lesson 5: Life Skills • Read and write numbers

A Match the words with the numbers.

1. fifteen _b_
2. twelve ____
3. eighteen ____
4. seventeen ____
5. ten ____
6. nineteen ____
7. fourteen ____
8. sixteen ____
9. eleven ____
10. thirteen ____

a. 18
b. 15
c. 13
d. 11
e. 16
f. 19
g. 17
h. 12
i. 10
j. 14

B Read the words. Write the numbers.

1. twenty-five _25_
2. thirty-seven _____
3. sixty-two _____
4. seventy _____
5. ninety-eight _____
6. one hundred _____

7. seventy-four _____
8. forty-nine _____
9. fifty-one _____
10. eighty-four _____
11. forty-three _____
12. ninety-six _____

C Read the schedules. Complete the sentences.

1. Mai's class is _____ _two_ _____ hours.

2. Her break is _____ minutes.

3. Dawit's class is _____ hours.

4. His break is _____ minutes.

Mai's Schedule

Class: 10:30 A.M.–12:30 P.M.

Break: 11:45 A.M.–11:55 P.M.

Dawit's Schedule

Class: 5:00 P.M.–8:00 P.M.

Break: 6:30 P.M.–6:50 P.M.

D Look at the numbers. Write the words. Use the words in the box.

eighty-six   fifty-nine   fourteen   one hundred   sixty
eleven   forty-seven   ninety   ~~seventy-one~~   thirty-three

1. 71 _____seventy-one_____

2. 59 _____

3. 11 _____

4. 60 _____

5. 33 _____

6. 14 _____

7. 100 _____

8. 90 _____

9. 47 _____

10. 86 _____

E Play Track 21. Listen for the time. Circle *a*, *b*, or *c*.

1. a. 5:55   (b.) 5:15   c. 5:50

2. a. 6:08   b. 6:28   c. 6:18

3. a. 4:20   b. 4:12   c. 4:22

4. a. 2:33   b. 2:13   c. 2:30

F Play Track 22. Listen. Write the number.

1. _93_   3. _____   5. _____   7. _____

2. _____   4. _____   6. _____   8. _____

A 🖸 Play Track 23. Listen to the story.
Number the sentences in the correct order.

_____ He gets to work at 6:50. He starts work at 7:00.

_____ He is always early for class.

_1_ Carlo likes to be on time.

_____ On weekends, Carlo meets friends.
He is always late!

_____ He gets up early and gets ready for work.

_____ Carlo goes to school after work.

B Read the sentences in Exercise A again.
Write the sentences in the correct order.

1. _Carlo likes to be on time._ _____

2. _____

3. _____

4. _____

5. _____

6. _____

C 🖸 Play Track 23 again to check your answers to Exercise B.

Phonics: The sounds of *d* and *t*

A Play Track 24. Listen. Write *d* or *t*.

1. _d_ inner
2. ____wenty
3. ____ime
4. ____on't
5. fif____een
6. ____wo
7. Thurs____ay
8. Sun____ay
9. Mon____ay
10. ge____ ____ressed
11. ea____ breakfas____
12. ____wenty-____wo

B Play Track 25. Listen. Write the words.

1. _____dinner_____
2. _____
3. _____
4. _____
5. _____
6. _____
7. _____
8. _____
9. _____
10. _____

Lesson 1: Family members

A Look at the pictures. Circle *a* or *b*.

1. (a.) brother
   b. sister

2. a. grandmother
   b. grandfather

3. a. father
   b. mother

4. a. daughter
   b. son

5. a. children
   b. parents

6. a. wife
   b. husband

7. a. children
   b. parents

8. a. father
   b. son

9. a. grandfather
   b. sister

B 🔘 **Play Track 26. Listen. Write the missing words.**
Use the words in the box.

> brother   ~~father~~   grandmother   mother   son
> daughter   grandfather   husband   sister   wife

1. **A:** Who's that?

   B: That's my ____father____ .

2. **A:** Who's that?

   B: That's my _____ .

3. **A:** Who's that?

   B: That's my _____ .

4. **A:** Who's that?

   B: That's my _____ .

5. **A:** Who's that?

   B: That's my _____ .

6. **A:** Who's that?

   B: That's my _____ .

7. **A:** Who's that?

   B: That's my _____ .

8. **A:** Who's that?

   B: That's my _____ .

9. **A:** Who's that?

   B: That's my _____ .

10. **A:** Who's that?

    B: That's my _____ .

A Read the story.

> This is Antonio and his family. His wife is Beatriz. Antonio has two sons. Their names are Luis and Mario. He has one daughter. Her name is Marisa.

B Read the story again. Circle *a* or *b.*

1. Beatriz is Antonio's ____.

   a. wife   b. daughter

2. Luis is Antonio's ____.

   a. father   b. son

3. Beatriz is Luis's ____.

   a. sister   b. mother

4. Mario is Marisa's ____.

   a. brother   b. father

5. Antonio is Mario's ____.

   a. father   b. brother

6. Mario is Luis's ____.

   a. father   b. brother

7. Marisa is Beatriz's ____.

   a. sister   b. daughter

8. Antonio is Marisa's ____.

   a. father   b. son

C Read the questions. Circle *Yes* or *No.*

1. Do you have any sisters?   Yes   No

2. Do you have any brothers?   Yes   No

3. Do you have any children?   Yes   No

D Complete the chart. Use the words in the box.

~~parent~~   brother   grandparents   son   daughter   sons   child
sister   ~~parents~~   brothers   daughters   children   sisters   grandparent

Singular	Plural
parent	parents

E Complete the sentences. Use the words in the box.

brothers   children   grandparents   parents   ~~sisters~~

1. My sister Pam and my sister Meg are my _____ *sisters* _____.

2. My mother and father are my _____.

3. My grandmother and grandfather are my _____.

4. My brother David and my brother Tony are my _____.

5. My son and daughter are my _____.

A Look at the pictures. Write the household chores.
Use the words in the box.

> clean the house   make dinner   wash the dishes
> do the laundry   take out the garbage ~~vacuum~~

1. *vacuum*

2. _____

3. _____

4. _____

5. _____

6. _____

B Write the questions. Complete the answers.
Use the correct form of the verbs in parentheses.

1. (vacuum)

   A: _Who vacuums?_

   B: My father _____ vacuums _____.

2. (make dinner)

   A: _____

   B: My sister _____.

3. (take out the garbage)

   A: _____

   B: My son _____.

4. (clean the house)

   A: _____

   B: My mother _____.

5. (do the laundry)

   A: _____

   B: My brother _____.

6. (wash the dishes)

   A: _____

   B: My daughter _____.

C Check (✓) the chores you do at home.

☐ clean the house   ☐ take out the garbage

☐ do the laundry   ☐ wash the dishes

☐ make dinner   ☐ vacuum

A Write the months in order.

> April   December   ~~January~~   June   May   October
> August   February   July   March   November   September

1. _____January_____   7. _____

2. _____   8. _____

3. _____   9. _____

4. _____   10. _____

5. _____   11. _____

6. _____   12. _____

B 🔵 Play Track 27. Listen for the ordinal number. Circle *a* or *b.*

1. a. first   (b.) second   4. a. eighth   b. eighteenth

2. a. seventh   b. seventeenth   5. a. twenty-second   b. twenty-seventh

3. a. fifth   b. fifteenth   6. a. thirteenth   b. thirtieth

A Write the number or the month.

Number	Month	Number	Month
_1_	January	___	July
2	_February_	___	August
3	_____	9	_____
4	_____	10	_____
___	May	___	November
6	_____	12	_____

B Match the dates.

1. October 31, 2000 _i_   a. 12/25/82
2. August 4, 1990 ____   b. 2/14/06
3. December 25, 1982 ____   c. 3/17/73
4. February 14, 2006 ____   d. 8/4/90
5. March 17, 1973 ____   e. 6/10/05
6. May 27, 1950 ____   f. 11/21/65
7. September 30, 2010 ____   g. 4/7/12
8. November 21, 1965 ____   h. 5/27/50
9. April 7, 2012 ____   i. 10/31/00
10. June 10, 2005 ____   j. 9/30/10

C Write the missing numbers and words.

1. April 14, 1998   <u>4/14/98</u>

2. June 17, 1985   _____

3. September 1, 2007   _____

4. February 22,1974   _____

5. March 21, 2010   _____

6. _____   11/29/99

7. _____   7/13/02

8. _____   1/8/95

9. _____   10/19/68

10. _____   5/31/83

D Circle the month, day, or year.

4/**8**/05 = **month**	4/**8**/05 = **day**	4/8/**05** = **year**

1. Circle the month.   ⑥/20/93

2. Circle the day.   9/30/04

3. Circle the year.   12/6/72

4. Circle the month.   5/30/06

5. Circle the day.   10/17/58

6. Circle the year.   1/9/08

7. Circle the month.   2/25/80

8. Circle the day.   11/4/97

9. Circle the year.   4/2/03

April 2, 2008
4/2/08

A Read the sentences.

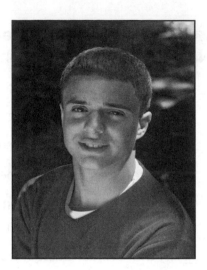

1. My first name is Pawel.
2. My middle name is Michal.
3. My last name is Jasinski.
4. I'm from Poland.
5. I was born on June 1, 1986.
6. I'm in ESL-2.
7. I go to English class on Tuesday and Thursday.
8. My teacher's name is Mrs. Johnson.
9. My class is from 2:00 to 5:00.
10. My class is in Room 12.

B Read the sentences again. Fill out the form.

Adult Education Center

Adult
Education
Center

Name	*Pawel*
	First Middle Last

Date of Birth		Place of Birth	

Class		Teacher	

Class Schedule	
	Day/s Time Room

A 🔘 **Play Track 28. Listen to the story.
Number the sentences in the correct order.**

_____ In their country, men go to work.

_____ Ernesto helps at home. He does the dishes.

_1_ Ernesto and Maria are married.

_____ Sometimes Ernesto goes to the supermarket, too.

_____ In their country, women stay at home.
They do all the household chores.

_____ In the United States, both Maria and Ernesto go to work.

B **Read the sentences in Exercise A again.
Write the sentences in the correct order.**

1. _Ernesto and Maria are married._

2. _____

3. _____

4. _____

5. _____

6. _____

C 🔘 **Play Track 28 again to check your answers to Exercise B.**

A 🔊 Play Track 29. Listen. Write *d* or *th*.

1. __d__ishes

2. ____ird

3. ____ate

4. mo____er

5. husban____

6. ____aughter

7. ____ere

8. laun____ry

9. bro____er

10. gran____fa____er

11. ____irteen____

12. gran____mo____er

FEBRUARY						
Sunday	Monday	Tuesday	Wednesday	Thursday	Friday	Saturday
1	2	③	4	5	6	7
8	9	10	11	12	13	14
15	16	17	18	19	20	21
22	23	24	25	26	27	28

B 🔊 Play Track 30. Listen. Write the words.

1. _____dishes_____

2. _____

3. _____

4. _____

5. _____

6. _____

7. _____

8. _____

9. _____

10. _____

Lesson 1: Make change with U.S. coins

A Match the pictures with the words.

a.

b.

c.

d.

e.

f.

1. a dime __b__

2. a quarter ____

3. a dollar coin ____

4. a penny ____

5. a half-dollar ____

6. a nickel ____

B Read the words. Write the coins. Use the words in the box.

> a dime   a dollar coin   a half-dollar   a nickel   ~~a quarter~~

1. Two dimes and one nickel = _____ *a quarter* _____

2. Five pennies = _____

3. Two quarters = _____

4. Five pennies and one nickel = _____

5. Three quarters, two dimes, and one nickel = _____

C Look at the pictures. Complete the sentences.

1.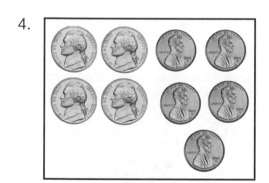

   A: Do you have change for a dollar?

   B: Yes. I have a _____quarter_____,

   six _____dimes_____, and

   three _____nickels_____.

2.

   A: Do you have change for a quarter?

   B: Yes. I have two _____ and

   a _____.

3.

   A: Do you have change for a dollar?

   B: Yes. I have three _____,

   two _____, and

   a _____.

4.

   A: Do you have change for a quarter?

   B: Yes. I have four _____ and

   five _____.

5.

   A: Do you have change for a dollar?

   B: Yes. I have two _____ and

   five _____.

Lesson 2: Make change with U.S. bills

A Look at the pictures. Write the amount. Use the words in the box.

> fifty   five   one   one hundred   ~~ten~~   twenty

1. ____ten____ dollars

2. _____ dollars

3. _____ dollars

4. _____ dollars

5. _____ dollars

6. _____ dollar

B Look at the pictures. Write the amount. Use the words in the box.

fifty dollars   one hundred dollars   ten dollars   ~~twenty dollars~~

1. _twenty dollars_

2. _____

3. _____

4. _____

C 🎵 Play Track 31. Listen. Write the missing words.

1. **A:** Do you have change for a _____ _five_ _____?

   B: Yes. I have five _____ _singles_ _____.

2. **A:** Do you have change for a _____?

   B: Yes. I have a twenty and three _____.

3. **A:** Do you have change for a _____?

   B: Yes. I have a _____ and five singles.

4. **A:** Do you have change for a _____?

   B: Yes. I have a fifty, a _____, and three tens.

A Look at the pictures. Write the words. Use the words in the box.

aspirin	lightbulbs	shampoo	tissues
batteries	paper towels	shaving cream	toilet paper
deodorant	razor blades	soap	~~toothpaste~~

1. _toothpaste_

2. _____

3. _____

4. _____

5. _____

6. _____

7. _____

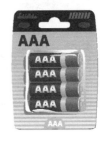

8. _____

9. _____

10. _____

11. _____

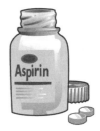

12. _____

B Circle *is* or *are.*

1. Where _____ the toilet paper?   (is)   are
2. Where _____ the razor blades?   is   are
3. Where _____ the deodorant?   is   are
4. Where _____ the toothpaste?   is   are
5. Where _____ the lightbulbs?   is   are
6. Where _____ the paper towels?   is   are
7. Where _____ the shaving cream?   is   are
8. Where _____ the shampoo?   is   are

C Write *Where is* or *Where are.*

1. **A:** Excuse me. _Where is_ the soap?

   B: Aisle 2.

   A: Thank you.

2. **A:** Excuse me. _____ the tissues?

   B: Aisle 3.

   A: Thank you.

3. **A:** Excuse me. _____ the batteries?

   B: Aisle 1.

   A: Thank you.

4. **A:** Excuse me. _____ the toilet paper?

   B: Aisle 4.

   A: Thank you.

5. **A:** Excuse me. _____ the aspirin?

   B: Aisle 5.

   A: Thank you.

Lesson 4: Ask for and give prices

A Look at the pictures. Circle *a* or *b*.

1.

(a.) $5.76   b. $5.56

2.

a. $13.10   b. $13.20

3.

a. $25.14   b. $25.12

4.

a. $60.30   b. $65.30

5.

a. $36.02   b. $36.20

B 🔘 Play Track 32. Listen. Write the prices.

1. __22¢__   3. _____   5. _____

2. _____   4. _____   6. _____

C 🔘 Play Track 33. Listen. Write the prices.

1. __$1.59__   3. _____   5. _____

2. _____   4. _____   6. _____

D 🔘 Play Track 34. Listen. Write the prices.

1.

2.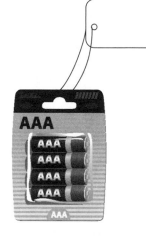

3.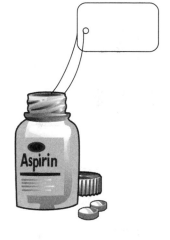

4.

5.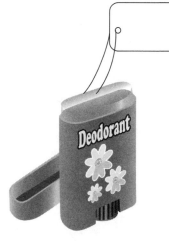

6.

A Read the receipt.

```
              City Drugstore

                    Date: 04/12/10


1 Toilet paper                 $1.79
1 Deodorant                     2.79
1 Tissues                       1.50
1 Aspirin                       6.29
1 Batteries                     5.19

Transaction Total:

5 items   Subtotal           $17.56
              Tax              1.44
              Total         $19.00

Paid by: Cash                $20.00
Change                        $1.00
```

B Read the receipt again. Circle *Yes* or *No.*

1. The name of the store is City Drugstore.   Yes   No

2. The date on the receipt is December 4, 2010.   Yes   No

3. The aspirin is $6.09.   Yes   No

4. The subtotal is $20.00.   Yes   No

5. The change is $1.00.   Yes   No

C Read the receipt again. Write the prices.

1. How much is the toilet paper? $1.79

2. How much is the deodorant? _____

3. How much are the batteries? _____

4. How much is the tax? _____

5. How much is the total? _____

D Fill out the checks. Use the words in each box.

$15.50   ~~City Drugstore~~   Fifteen dollars and $\frac{50}{100}$

June 20, 2010   Tom Jones

```
                                                              335

                                        DATE _____

PAY TO THE
ORDER OF   City Drugstore _____   $ _____

IN THE AMOUNT OF _____ DOLLARS

Brookside Bank
4 Main Street
New York, NY 10001

MEMO _____        _____
693657264    9847    335
```

$35.15   ~~City Drugstore~~   Martin Chen

May 14, 2010   Thirty-five dollars and $\frac{15}{100}$

```
                                                              336
                                        DATE _____

PAY TO THE   City Drugstore _____   $ _____
ORDER OF

IN THE AMOUNT OF _____ DOLLARS

Madison Bank
18 Park Avenue
Los Angeles, CA 90001

MEMO _____        _____
693658925    1056    336
```

A 🎧 **Play Track 35. Listen to the story.**
Number the sentences in the correct order.

____ I get good bargains.

_1_ My name is Edna. In my country, I shop at markets.

____ How do I get good bargains?
I buy things on sale!

____ I pay the price on the price tag.

____ I talk to the salespeople about the prices.

____ In the United States, I shop in big stores.

B Read the sentences in Exercise A again.
Write the sentences in the correct order.

1. _My name is Edna. In my country, I shop at markets._

2. _____

3. _____

4. _____

5. _____

6. _____

C 🎧 **Play Track 35 again to check your answers to Exercise B.**

A 🔘 Play Track 36. Listen. Write *g* or *c*.

1. _g_ o

2. shaving ____ream

3. bi____

4. ____ountry

5. ____et

6. ____omputer

7. price ta____

8. ____ount

9. ____ood

10. dru____store

11. ____ash

12. ____oin

B 🔘 Play Track 37. Listen. Write the words.

1. _____go_____   6. _____

2. _____   7. _____

3. _____   8. _____

4. _____   9. _____

5. _____   10. _____

A Look at the pictures. Complete the words.

1. t<u> o </u>ma<u> t </u>o<u> e </u>s

2. o____io____s

3. ____ucu____be____s

4. mu____h____o____ms

5. ____e____s

6. c____r____ots

7. le____t____ce

8. ____ep____ers

9. p____t____to____s

B 🔘 **Play Track 38. Listen for the vegetables. Circle *a* or *b*.**

1. (a.) tomatoes and onions   b. potatoes and onions

2. a. peppers and mushrooms   b. peas and mushrooms

3. a. carrots and lettuce   b. cucumbers and lettuce

4. a. potatoes and peppers   b. potatoes and peas

5. a. cucumbers and onions   b. carrots and onions

6. a. tomatoes and peas   b. tomatoes and peppers

C **Read the story.**

Beata needs to make dinner. She wants to make chicken and vegetables. She has chicken, onions, and peas. She needs potatoes, carrots, and mushrooms. Her son goes to the store. He buys the vegetables. Beata makes dinner. It's delicious!

D **Read the story again. Circle *a* or *b*.**

1. Beata wants to make ____.

   a. lunch   (b.) dinner

2. She wants to make ____.

   a. chicken and carrots   b. chicken and vegetables

3. She has chicken, ____, and peas.

   a. mushrooms   b. onions

4. Beata needs potatoes, carrots, and ____.

   a. mushrooms   b. onions

5. Her ____ goes to the store.

   a. husband   b. son

6. He buys ____.

   a. potatoes, carrots, and mushrooms   b. potatoes, carrots, and onions

A Look at the pictures. Complete the sentences.
Use *like* and *don't like* and the words in the box.

carrots	lettuce	peas	~~potatoes~~
cucumbers	onions	~~peppers~~	tomatoes

1. I _____ like potatoes _____ .

   I _____ don't like peppers _____ .

2. We _____ .

   We _____ .

3. They _____ .

   They _____ .

4. Bernard and Sue _____ .

   They _____ .

B Play Track 39. Listen. Write the vegetables.

1. **A:** Do you like vegetables?

   B: I like _____peas_____ . I don't like _____onions_____ .

2. **A:** Do you like vegetables?

   B: I like _____ . I don't like _____ .

3. **A:** Do you like vegetables?

   B: I like _____ . I don't like _____ .

4. **A:** Do you like vegetables?

   B: I like _____ . I don't like _____ .

C Answer the questions. Use true or made-up information. Circle *Yes* or *No*. Then write a sentence. Use the example below as a model.

   Do you like peas?

   (Yes)   No   _I like peas._____

1. Do you like lettuce?

   Yes   No   _____

2. Do you like cucumbers?

   Yes   No   _____

3. Do you like carrots?

   Yes   No   _____

4. Do you like peppers?

   Yes   No   _____

5. Do you like mushrooms?

   Yes   No   _____

6. Do you like potatoes?

   Yes   No   _____

7. Do you like onions?

   Yes   No   _____

A Look at the pictures. Write the names of the fruit.
Use the words in the box.

~~apples~~	grapes	peaches
bananas	mangoes	pears
cherries	oranges	strawberries

1. _____apples_____   2. _____   3. _____

4. _____   5. _____   6. _____

7. _____   8. _____   9. _____

B Read the questions. Complete the answers.

1. **A:** Does Tom like bananas?

   B: Yes. He _____likes_____ bananas.

2. **A:** Does Maria like strawberries?

   B: Yes. She _____ strawberries.

3. **A:** Does Luke like peaches?

   B: No. He _____ peaches.

4. **A:** Does Meg like cherries?

   B: Yes. She _____ cherries.

5. **A:** Does Sarah like grapes?

   B: No. She _____ grapes.

6. **A:** Does John like apples?

   B: No. He _____ apples.

C Look at the pictures. Complete the sentences. Use *like* and *doesn't like*.

1. Marie _likes grapes_____.

2. Yao _____.

3. Roberto's sister _____.

4. Eva _____.

5. My father _____.

6. My teacher _____.

A Look at the pictures. Write the words. Use the words in the box.

a bag of rice ~~a can of soup~~ a gallon of milk
a box of cereal a dozen eggs a loaf of bread

1. _____a can of soup_____   2. _____

3. _____   4. _____

5. _____   6. _____

B Write the plural form of the words in parentheses.

1. **A:** What do we need from the store?

   B: We need two (gallon) _____gallons_____ of milk and

   two (box) _____ of cereal.

2. **A:** What do we need from the store?

   B: We need four (pound) _____ of chicken and

   three (bag) _____ of rice.

3. **A:** What do we need from the store?

   B: We need two (loaf) _____ of bread and

   three (box) _____ of cereal.

4. **A:** What do we need from the store?

   B: We need three (pound) _____ of fish and

   five (can) _____ of soup.

C Look at the pictures. Complete the sentences.

1.

   A: Do you need anything from the store?

   B: Yes. I need a ____loaf of bread____ and

   two ____gallons of milk____.

2.

   A: Do you need anything from the store?

   B: Yes. I need a _____ and

   two _____.

3.

   A: Do you need anything from the store?

   B: Yes. I need two _____ and

   three _____.

4.

   A: Do you need anything from the store?

   B: Yes. I need a _____ and

   two _____.

A Read the shopping ad.

B Read the shopping ad again. Write the prices.

1. How much is a loaf of bread? $1.59

2. How much is one pound of fish? _____

3. How much are four cans of soup? _____

4. How much is a box of cereal? _____

5. How much are two dozen eggs? _____

C Look at the pictures. Write a shopping list.

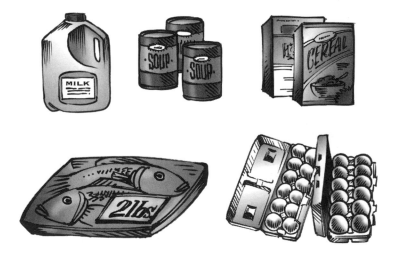

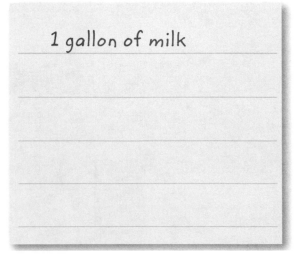

1 gallon of milk

A Match the pictures with the words.

 a.

 b.

 c.

 d.

e.

f.

1. milk _d_

2. pancakes ____

3. cereal ____

4. eggs and toast ____

5. juice ____

6. tea ____

B Play Track 40. Listen for the menu items. Circle *a* or *b*.

1. (a.)    b.

2. a.   b.

3. a.   b.

4. a.   b.

5. a.   b.

A 🔊 Play Track 41. Listen to the story.
Number the sentences in the correct order.

_____ Sometimes children eat with their fingers.

_____ How do you eat in your country?

_____ My name is Kyoko.
In my country, people usually drink their soup.

_1_ My name is Tran.
In my country, people usually eat with chopsticks.

_____ In the United States, people usually eat with forks, knives, and spoons.

_____ Sometimes they eat food with their fingers, like sandwiches and French fries.

B Read the sentences in Exercise A again.
Write the sentences in the correct order.

1. _My name is Tran. In my country, people usually eat with chopsticks._

2. _____

3. _____

4. _____

5. _____

6. _____

C 🔊 Play Track 41 again to check your answers to Exercise B.

A 🔘 Play Track 42. Listen. Write *f* or *v*.

1. __f__ruit

2. ____egetables

3. ____ery

4. ____ood

5. ____ish

6. ha____e

7. bee____

8. co____fee

9. li____e

10. ____i____teen

11. ____i____e

12. ____a____orite

B 🔘 Play Track 43. Listen. Write the words.

1. _____fruit_____   6. _____

2. _____   7. _____

3. _____   8. _____

4. _____   9. _____

5. _____   10. _____

Lesson 1: Rooms in a home

A Look at the picture. Write the rooms. Use the words in the box.

basement	~~bedroom~~	dining room	kitchen	living room
bathroom	closet	garage	laundry room	

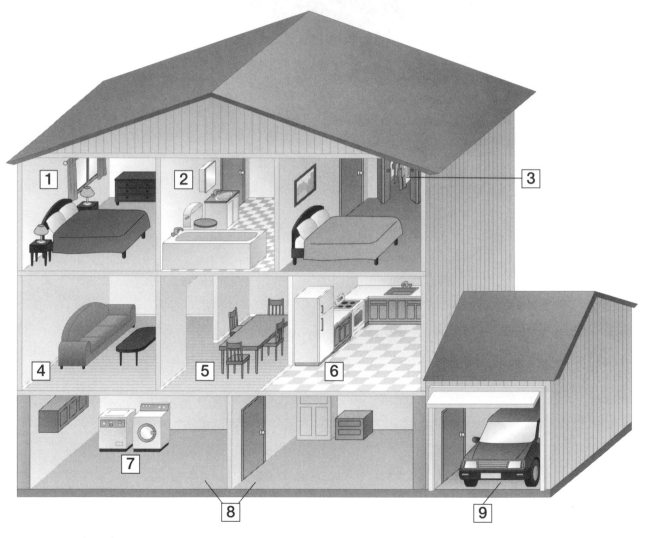

1. ___bedroom___

2. _____

3. _____

4. _____

5. _____

6. _____

7. _____

8. _____

9. _____

B Look at the apartment. Write the rooms.

A: Guess what? I have a new apartment.

B: Really? What's it like?

A: It has two ___bedrooms___, two _____, a _____,

and a _____.

B: It sounds great!

C Read the story.

> My name is Marcus. I have a new apartment. It has two bedrooms, one bathroom, a living room, and a kitchen. It's great!

D Read the story again. Circle *Yes* or *No*.

1. The apartment has two bedrooms.   (Yes)   No
2. It has two bathrooms.   Yes   No
3. It has a living room.   Yes   No
4. It has a dining room.   Yes   No
5. It has a kitchen.   Yes   No
6. It has a laundry room.   Yes   No

A Match the pictures with the words.

a.    b.    c.    d.

1. sunny _c_

2. modern ____

3. large ____

4. small ____

B Play Track 44. Listen. Write the missing words.

1. **A:** Can you tell me about the apartment for rent?

    B: There is a _____sunny_____ living room and a _____ kitchen.

    A: It sounds nice.

2. **A:** Can you tell me about the apartment for rent?

    B: There is a _____ garage and a _____ dining room.

    A: It sounds nice.

3. **A:** Can you tell me about the apartment for rent?

    B: There is a _____ closet and a _____ basement.

    A: It sounds nice.

4. **A:** Can you tell me about the apartment for rent?

    B: There is a _____ bedroom and a _____ kitchen.

    A: It sounds nice.

5. **A:** Can you tell me about the apartment for rent?

    B: There is a _____ kitchen and a _____ bathroom.

    A: It sounds nice.

C Circle *is* or *are.*

1. There ____ one bedroom.   (is)   are
2. There ____ five bedrooms.   is   are
3. There ____ three closets.   is   are
4. There ____ a large kitchen.   is   are
5. There ____ a modern bathroom.   is   are
6. There ____ four sunny bedrooms.   is   are
7. There ____ a large garage.   is   are
8. There ____ a laundry room.   is   are
9. There ____ two large bathrooms.   is   are
10. There ____ a small kitchen.   is   are

D Write *There is* or *There are.*

1. _____There is_____ a modern kitchen.

2. _____ four bathrooms.

3. _____ a large living room.

4. _____ a large basement.

5. _____ two small bedrooms.

6. _____ a modern dining room.

7. _____ six closets.

8. _____ a large laundry room.

9. _____ a sunny kitchen.

10. _____ four large closets.

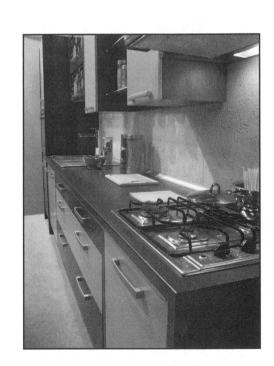

A Look at the pictures. Write the words. Use the words in the box.

bed	dishwasher	dryer	refrigerator	sofa	table
chair	dresser	lamp	sink	stove	~~washing machine~~

1. *washing machine*

2. _____

3. _____

4. _____

5. _____

6. _____

7. _____

8. _____

9. _____

10. _____

11. _____

12. _____

B Complete the questions and answers.

1. **A:** _____Is there_____ a sink?

   B: Yes, _____there is_____.

2. **A:** _____ any tables?

   B: No, _____.

3. **A:** _____ any chairs?

   B: No, _____.

4. **A:** _____ a dryer?

   B: No, _____.

5. **A:** _____ any beds?

   B: Yes, _____.

6. **A:** _____ a washing machine?

   B: Yes, _____.

C Play Track 45. Listen. Circle *a* or *b*.

1. (a.) There is a stove in the apartment.

   b. There isn't a stove in the apartment.

2. a. There are lamps in the apartment.

   b. There aren't any lamps in the apartment.

3. a. There are chairs in the apartment.

   b. There aren't any chairs in the apartment.

4. a. There is a washing machine in the apartment.

   b. There isn't a washing machine in the apartment.

5. a. There are tables in the apartment.

   b. There aren't any tables in the apartment.

6. a. There is a bed in the apartment.

   b. There isn't a bed in the apartment.

A **Look at the pictures. Complete the addresses.**

1. __14__ Cherry Lane

2. 1498 _____ Street

3. 5 City _____

4. 910 _____ _____

5. _____ _____ Avenue

6. _____ Lake _____

7. _____ Cherry _____

8. _____ _____ _____

B Read the apartment ads. Circle *a* or *b.*

For rent
1 bedroom
459 Orange Avenue
$675/month

1. What's the address?
   (a.) 459 Orange Avenue   b. $675/month
2. How much is the rent?
   a. 459 Orange Avenue   b. $675/month

For rent
3 bedrooms
1326 Cedar Lane
$995/month

3. What's the address?
   a. 1326 Cedar Lane   b. $995/month
4. How much is the rent?
   a. 1326 Cedar Lane   b. $995/month

For rent
2 bedrooms
15 Ocean Drive
$850/month

5. What's the address?
   a. 15 Ocean Drive   b. $850/month
6. How much is the rent?
   a. 15 Ocean Drive   b. $850/month

C Play Track 46. Listen. Complete the addresses.

1. __13__ Martin Street
2. _____ Angelo Drive
3. _____ Green Boulevard
4. _____ South Lane
5. _____ Meadow Road
6. _____ Erie Avenue

A Match the words with the abbreviations.

1. Street __d__   a. Ln.
2. Drive ____   b. Ave.
3. Boulevard ____   c. Rd.
4. Apartment ____   d. St.
5. Road ____   e. Blvd.
6. Lane ____   f. Apt.
7. Avenue ____   g. Dr.

B Look at the envelope. Circle *Yes* or *No*.

Maria Hernandez
874 Apple Dr.
Middletown, NJ 07748

Hong Li
14 Lake Drive
Chicago, IL 60647

1. The letter is from Maria Hernandez.   (Yes)   No
2. Maria's last name is Hernandez.   Yes   No
3. The return address is 14 Lake Drive.   Yes   No
4. Ms. Hernandez lives in Middletown.   Yes   No
5. Ms. Hernandez's zip code is 60647.   Yes   No

C Look at the envelope again. Where is it going? Circle *Yes* or *No.*

Maria Hernandez
874 Apple Dr.
Middletown, NJ 07748

Hong Li
14 Lake Drive
Chicago, IL 60647

1. The letter is going to Mr. Li.   (Yes)   No
2. Mr. Li's first name is Hong.   Yes   No
3. The letter is going to 874 Apple Drive.   Yes   No
4. Mr. Li lives in Chicago.   Yes   No
5. Mr. Li's zip code is 07748.   Yes   No

D Write your answers. Use true or made-up information.

1. What's your first name?   _____

2. What's your last name?   _____

3. What's your address?   _____

4. What's your city?   _____

5. What's your state?   _____

6. What's your zip code?   _____

A 🔘 Play Track 47. Listen to the story.
Number the sentences in the correct order.

_____ Alicia has a good job.

_____ But Alicia's parents are not happy.

_1_ Alicia is 21 years old.

_____ What should Alicia do?

_____ She is single.

_____ In their country, single people live with their families.

_____ Now she wants to move to an apartment with her friends.

_____ In the United States, single people often live alone or with friends.

_____ Alicia lives with her older sister and her brother-in-law in California.

B Read the sentences in Exercise A again. Write the story.

Alicia is 21 years old. _____

_____

_____

_____

_____

_____

C 🔘 Play Track 47 again to check your answers to Exercise B.

A Look at the pictures. Write *l* or *r.*

1. dishwashe_*r*_

2. dresse____

3. tab____e

4. chai____

5. ____efrigerato____

6. ____amp

B 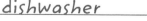 Play Track 48 to check your answers to Exercise A.

C  Play Track 49. Listen. Write the words.

1. _____dishwasher_____   6. _____

2. _____   7. _____

3. _____   8. _____

4. _____   9. _____

5. _____   10. _____

Lesson 1: Clothes and shoes

A Look at the pictures. Write the words. Use the words in the box.

a blouse	a jacket	pants	shoes	~~sneakers~~	a sweater
a dress	jeans	a shirt	a skirt	socks	a T-shirt

1. _____sneakers_____

2. _____

3. _____

4. _____

5. _____

6. _____

7. _____

8. _____

9. _____

10. _____

11. _____

12. _____

B 🎵 Play Track 50. Listen for the clothes and shoes. Circle *a, b,* or *c.*

1. a.    (b.)   c.

2. a.   b.   c.

3. a.    b.   c.

4. a.   b.   c.

5. a.   b.   c.

6. a.   b.    c.

C 🎵 Play Track 51. Listen. Write the missing words.

1. **A:** Let's go shopping! I need a new _____*jacket*_____.

   B: OK. I need _____*shoes*_____.

2. **A:** Let's go shopping! I need new _____.

   B: OK. I need a _____.

3. **A:** Let's go shopping! I need a new _____.

   B: OK. I need a _____.

4. **A:** Let's go shopping! I need new _____.

   B: OK. I need _____.

A Play Track 52. Listen. Write the missing words and numbers.

1. **A:** Can I help you?

    B: Do you have this shirt in a _____ large _____?

    A: Yes. Here you go.

    B: Do you have these sneakers in a size _____ 11 _____?

    A: I'm sorry. We don't.

2. **A:** Can I help you?

    B: Do you have this blouse in a _____?

    A: Yes. Here you go.

    B: Do you have these jeans in a size _____?

    A: I'm sorry. We don't.

3. **A:** Can I help you?

    B: Do you have this T-shirt in an _____?

    A: Yes. Here you go.

    B: Do you have these shoes in a size _____?

    A: I'm sorry. We don't.

B Write *This, this, These,* or *these.*

1. Do you have _____ this _____ shirt in a small?

2. We have _____ jacket in an extra large.

3. _____ shirts are medium.

4. _____ dress is a large.

5. Do you have _____ sneakers in a size 10?

C Write *That, that, Those,* or *those.*

1. Do you have _____*that*_____ skirt in a medium?

2. Do you have _____ pants in a size 2?

3. _____ shirt is a large.

4. _____ sneakers are a size 6.

5. We have _____ blouse in a small.

6. We have _____ socks in a size 4.

D Look at the pictures. Write *this, that, these,* or *those.*

1. We have _____*those*_____
   shirts in a large.

2. We have _____
   sweater in a small.

3. We have _____
   shoes in a size 11.

4. We have _____
   dress in a size 10.

A Complete the words for colors.

1. r _e_ _d_

2. g____e____n

3. ____r____nge

4. b____ow____

5. ____el____ow

6. b____u____

7. w____it____

8. ____la____k

9. ____urp____e

10. ____r____y

11. p____n____

12. b____ig____

B Write the correct colors.

1. Bananas are ____yellow____.

2. Oranges are _____.

3. Carrots are _____.

4. Peas are _____.

5. Strawberries are _____.

6. Cucumbers are _____.

7. Tomatoes are _____.

8. Lettuce is _____.

9. Cherries are _____.

10. Mangoes are _____.

C Play Track 53. Listen for the color. Circle *a* or *b*.

1. (a.) black   b. blue

2. a. red   b. orange

3. a. green   b. blue

4. a. beige   b. brown

5. a. white   b. yellow

6. a. pink   b. purple

7. a. green   b. gray

8. a. blue   b. brown

D Read the story.

Kevin and Sahra are at a department store. The department store has a sale today. Kevin needs a blue sweater and brown shoes. Sahra needs a green blouse and a white skirt. She needs black shoes, too.

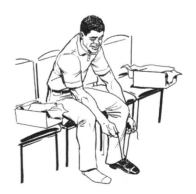

E Read the story again. Circle *Yes* or *No*.

1. Kevin and Sahra are at a department store.   (Yes)   No
2. Kevin needs a brown sweater.   Yes   No
3. Kevin needs black shoes.   Yes   No
4. Sahra needs a green blouse.   Yes   No
5. Sahra needs a blue skirt.   Yes   No
6. Sahra needs black shoes.   Yes   No

F Write your answers.

1. What color are your favorite sneakers? _____

2. What color are your favorite shoes?   _____

3. What color is your favorite sweater?   _____

4. What color is your favorite shirt?   _____

5. What color is your favorite T-shirt?   _____

6. What color is your favorite jacket?   _____

7. What color are your favorite pants?   _____

8. What color are your favorite jeans?   _____

G Write three things you are wearing. Include the colors.
Use the sentence below as a model.

I am wearing *a red shirt, beige pants, and brown shoes* .

I am wearing _____.

Ⓐ Look at the pictures. Write *big, long, short,* or *small.*

1. It's too _____small_____ .

2. They're too _____ .

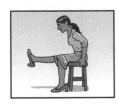

3. It's too _____ .

4. They're too _____ .

Ⓑ Look at the pictures. Then write sentences. Use *big, long, short,* or *small.*

1.  ___The jacket is too small._____

2. _____

3.  _____

4. _____

C Look at the pictures. Complete the sentences.
Write the clothes and the problems.

1.

A: I need to return a _____sweater_____ and some _____.

B: What's the problem?

A: The _____ is too _____ and the _____

are too _____. Here's my receipt.

2.

A: I need to return a _____ and some _____.

B: What's the problem?

A: The _____ is too _____ and the _____

are too _____. Here's my receipt.

D Play Track 54. Listen. Circle *a* or *b.*

1. a. The man needs to buy clothes.   (b.) The man needs to return clothes.

2. a. The sweater is too short.   b. The sweater is too long.

3. a. The sneakers are too small.   b. The sneakers are too big.

4. a. The man has a receipt.   b. The man doesn't have a receipt.

A Read the store ad.

CLOTHES WORLD SALE MAY 2–8

~~$45.00~~ / ON SALE $39.99

ALL SNEAKERS ON SALE

~~$29.99~~ / ON SALE $24.99

~~$45.00~~ / ON SALE $39.99

~~$40.00~~ / ON SALE $29.99

ALL SKIRTS ON SALE

B Read the ad again. Circle *Yes* or *No.*

1. The sale is at Clothes World.   (Yes)   No

2. The sale is May 2–May 9.   Yes   No

3. The sweater is on sale for $45.00.   Yes   No

4. The regular price of the jeans is $24.99.   Yes   No

5. The jacket is on sale for $39.99.   Yes   No

6. Men's shoes are on sale for $29.99.   Yes   No

C 🎵 Play Track 55. Listen. Write the correct answers from the box.

> 9:00 $15.50 $19.99 $25.00   ~~Clara's~~   Thursday

1. **A:** What store is having a sale?

   B: _____Clara's_____ Store is having a sale.

2. **A:** When is the sale?

   B: The sale is on _____.

3. **A:** What time does the store open?

   B: The store opens at _____.

4. **A:** How much are the jackets?

   B: The jackets are _____.

5. **A:** How much are the shoes?

   B: The shoes are _____.

6. **A:** How much are the shirts?

   B: The shirts are _____.

Lesson 6: Yun's story

A 🔘 Play Track 56. Listen to the story. Number the sentences in the correct order.

_____ In my country, people wear white for funerals.

_1_ My name is Yun.

_____ I want to wear a long white dress.

_____ What should I do?

_____ My wedding is in August.

_____ Women wear a red and green dress on their wedding day.

_____ My mother and grandmother want me to wear a red and green dress.

B Read the sentences in Exercise A again. Write the story.

My name is Yun.

_____

_____

_____

_____

_____

_____

_____

C 🔘 Play Track 56 again to check your answers to Exercise B.

A Look at the pictures. Write *s* or *sh.*

1. _s_kirt

2. ____irt

3. ____oes

4. ____weater

5. pant____

6. T-____irt

B Play Track 57 to check your answers to Exercise A.

C Play Track 58. Listen. Write the words.

1. _____skirt_____

6. _____

2. _____

7. _____

3. _____

8. _____

4. _____

9. _____

5. _____

10. _____

Unit 9: Our Busy Lives

Lesson 1: Free-time activities

A Match the pictures with the words.

a.

b.

c.

d.

e.

f.

g.

h.

i.

1. exercise _c_

2. read the newspaper ____

3. use e-mail ____

4. visit friends ____

5. go to the movies ____

6. listen to music ____

7. play the guitar ____

8. watch TV ____

9. play soccer ____

B Look at Sam's calendar. Circle *Yes* or *No.*

FEBRUARY

Sunday	Monday	Tuesday	Wednesday	Thursday	Friday	Saturday
1 visit friends	2 exercise	3 play soccer play the guitar	4 exercise	5 play the guitar	6 exercise	7 play soccer
8 visit friends	9 exercise	10 play soccer play the guitar	11 exercise	12 play the guitar	13 exercise	14 play soccer
15 visit friends	16 exercise	17 play soccer play the guitar	18 exercise	19 play the guitar	20 exercise	21 play soccer
22 visit friends	23 exercise	24 play soccer play the guitar	25 exercise	26 play the guitar	27 exercise	28 play soccer

1. Sam visits friends once a week.   (Yes)   No
2. He exercises three times a week.   Yes   No
3. He plays soccer three times a week.   Yes   No
4. Sam plays the guitar every Tuesday and Thursday.   Yes   No
5. He plays soccer every Monday and Friday.   Yes   No
6. He goes to the movies every Saturday.   Yes   No

C Write about yourself. Answer the questions.

1. What do you do in your free time? _____

_____

2. How often? _____

_____

Lesson 2: Present continuous

A Complete the sentences. Use the words in parentheses. Use the correct verb form.

1. **A:** Hello?

   B: Hi, Joe. Are you busy?

   A: I'm (play / the guitar) _playing the guitar_.

   Can I call you later?

   B: No problem. Bye.

   A: Goodbye.

2. **A:** Hello?

   B: Hi, Maria. Are you busy?

   A: I'm (go / to the library) _____.

   Can I call you later?

   B: No problem. Bye.

   A: Goodbye.

3. **A:** Hello?

   B: Hi, Susan. Are you busy?

   A: I'm (read / the newspaper) _____.

   Can I call you later?

   B: No problem. Bye.

   A: Goodbye.

4. **A:** Hello?

   B: Hi, Mark. Are you busy?

   A: I'm (go / to the movies) _____.

   Can I call you later?

   B: No problem. Bye.

   A: Goodbye.

B Rewrite the sentences. Use contractions.

1. She is using e-mail. *She's using e-mail.*

2. You are reading the newspaper. _____

3. They are watching TV. _____

4. We are listening to music. _____

5. He is going to the movies. _____

6. I am playing soccer. _____

7. She is exercising. _____

8. You are visiting friends. _____

9. I am playing the guitar. _____

C Write sentences. Use the present continuous. Use contractions.

1. (He / play soccer) *He's playing soccer.*

2. (We / go to the movies) _____

3. (I / read the newspaper) _____

4. (He / exercise) _____

5. (They / use e-mail) _____

6. (You / watch TV) _____

7. (She / play the guitar) _____

8. (I / visit friends) _____

9. (She / listen to music) _____

A Look at the pictures. Write the household chores. Use the words in the box.

clean the house	make dinner	~~talk on the phone~~
do homework	pay bills	walk the dog
do the laundry	take out the garbage	wash the car

1. _talk on the phone_

2. _____

3. _____

4. _____

5. _____

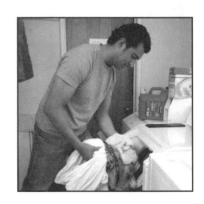

6. _____

7. _____

8. _____

9. _____

B Read the questions. Complete the answers. Use contractions.

1. Is he doing the laundry?   Yes, _____*he is*_____.

2. Is he washing the car?   No, _____.

3. Is she talking on the phone?   Yes, _____.

4. Are you walking the dog?   No, _____.

5. Are they making dinner?   Yes, _____.

6. Are the students doing homework?   No, _____.

C Write the questions.

1. (you / wash the car) *Are you washing the car?* _____

2. (Darya / pay bills) _____

3. (Ivan and Sara / study English) _____

4. (they / clean the house) _____

5. (he / take out the garbage) _____

6. (Ya-Wen / play soccer) _____

D Write about yourself. Answer the questions.

1. Are you doing homework? _____

2. Are you talking on the phone? _____

3. Are you studying English? _____

4. Are you writing? _____

A Look at the pictures. Write the workplace activities. Use the words in the box.

> answer the phone   ~~fix cars~~   take a break
> count money   help a customer   take orders
> drive a truck   look for something   work on the computer

1. ___fix cars___

2. _____

3. _____

4. _____

5. _____

6. _____

7. _____

8. _____

9. _____

B Write *he's, she's, I'm,* or *they're* and *not.*

1. **A:** Is he working on the computer?

   B: No, _____*he's not*_____ working on the computer. He's helping a customer.

2. **A:** Are they fixing cars?

   B: No, _____ fixing cars. They're counting money.

3. **A:** Are you taking a break?

   B: No, _____ taking a break. I'm taking orders.

4. **A:** Is she driving a truck?

   B: No, _____ driving a truck. She's looking for something.

5. **A:** Is he helping a customer?

   B: No, _____ helping a customer. He's taking orders.

C Look at the pictures. Write sentences. Use contractions.

1.  *She's not driving a truck.* _____

2.  _____

3.  _____

4.  _____

A Read the sentences. Complete the phone message.

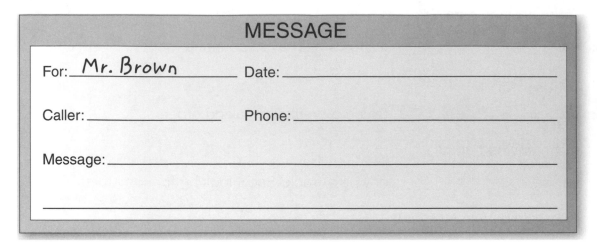

MESSAGE

For: *Mr. Brown*   Date: _____

Caller: _____   Phone: _____

Message: _____

1. The phone message is for Mr. Brown.
2. The date is March 14.
3. The caller is Carlos Rivera.
4. His phone number is 718-555-3746.
5. He's not coming to school today.

B Read the sentences. Complete the phone message.

MESSAGE

For: _____   Date: _____

Caller: _____   Phone: _____

Message: _____

1. The phone message is for Mrs. Smith.
2. The date is September 4.
3. The caller is Jane Reynolds.
4. Her phone number is 857-555-3854.
5. She's not coming to work today.

C 🔘 **Play Track 59. Listen. Complete the phone messages.**

1.

MESSAGE	
For: _Mr. Clark_	Date: _December 2_
Caller: _Marisa Costas_	Phone: _212-555-6798_
Message: _She's not coming to work today._	

2.

MESSAGE	
For: _Kyoko_	Date: _March 19_
Caller: _Ann_	Phone: _____
Message: _____	

3.

MESSAGE	
For: _Ms. Popova_	Date: _February 8_
Caller: _Sam White_	Phone: _____
Message: _____	

A 🔘 Play Track 60. Listen to the story.
Number the sentences in the correct order.

_____ They talk on the phone and go shopping.

_____ Then they spend time relaxing and talking.

_____ What do you do on weekends?

_____ On weekends, my wife and I eat alone.

_____ They play sports and watch TV.

_1_ My name is Alfonso.

_____ Our children don't sit down with us to eat.

_____ I have two children.

_____ They are busy every weekend with their friends.

_____ Do you spend time with your family or friends?

_____ In my country, families eat together on weekends.

B Read the sentences in Exercise A again. Write the story.

My name is Alfonso. _____

_____

_____

_____

_____

_____

C 🔘 Play Track 60 again to check your answers to Exercise B.

Phonics: The sounds of *a* (*date*) and *e* (*yes*)

A 🔵 Play Track 61. Listen. Write *a* or *e*.

1. m_e_ssage

2. d____te

3. h____lp

4. t____ke

5. n____me

6. ____very

7. tod____y

8. h____llo

9. ____xercise

10. newsp____per

11. W____dnesd____y

12. s____nt____nce

MESSAGE

For:_____ Date:_____

Caller:_____ Phone:_____

Message:_____

_____

MESSAGE

For:_____ Date:_____

Caller:_____ Phone:_____

Message:_____

_____

B 🔵 Play Track 62. Listen. Write the words.

1. _____*message*_____

2. _____

3. _____

4. _____

5. _____

6. _____

7. _____

8. _____

9. _____

10. _____

Lesson 1: Places in the community

A Match the pictures with the words.

a.

b.

c.

d.

e.

f.

g.

h.

i.

1. a supermarket __c__
2. a drugstore ____
3. a restaurant ____

4. a hospital ____
5. a gas station ____
6. a bank ____

7. an ATM ____
8. a parking lot ____
9. a computer store ____

B Look at the map. Write the streets.

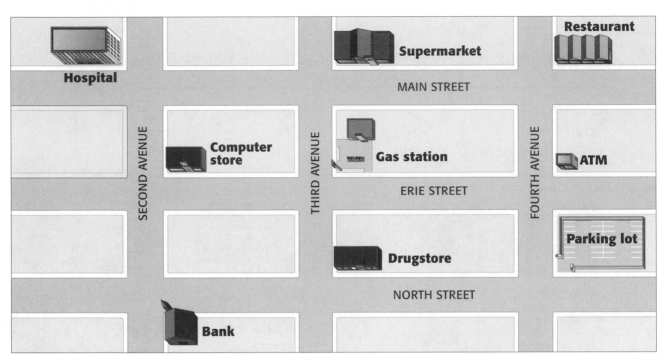

1. There's a parking lot on the corner of _North Street_ and _Fourth Avenue_.

2. There's a restaurant on the corner of _____ and _____.

3. There's a drugstore on the corner of _____ and _____.

4. There's a hospital on the corner of _____ and _____.

5. There's a computer store on the corner of _____ and _____.

6. There's a supermarket on the corner of _____ and _____.

7. There's a gas station on the corner of _____ and _____.

8. There's a bank on the corner of _____ and _____.

9. There's an ATM on the corner of _____ and _____.

A Look at the pictures. Write the places. Use the words in the box.

City Hall	fire station	police station
court house	library	~~post office~~
Department of Motor Vehicles (DMV)	park	school

1. _post office_

2. _____

3. _____

4. _____

5. _____

6. _____

7. _____

8. _____

9. _____

B Look at the map. Write *across from* or *between*.

| City Hall | DMV | Court house | Park |

MAIN STREET

| Police station | Hospital | Library | Post office |

1. **A:** Where is the park?

   B: It's _____across from_____ the post office.

2. **A:** Where is the library?

   B: It's _____ the court house.

3. **A:** Where is the court house?

   B: It's _____ the DMV and the park.

4. **A:** Where is City Hall?

   B: It's _____ the police station.

5. **A:** Where is the DMV?

   B: It's _____ City Hall and the court house.

6. **A:** Where is the post office?

   B: It's _____ the park.

7. **A:** Where is the police station?

   B: It's _____ City Hall.

8. **A:** Where is the hospital?

   B: It's _____ the police station and the library.

A Match the pictures with the words.

a.

b.

c.

d.

e.

f.

g.

h.

i.

1. walk _g_

2. take the subway ____

3. ride a bike ____

4. take a taxi ____

5. drive ____

6. take the bus ____

7. carpool ____

8. take the train ____

9. take a ferry ____

B 🔘 Play Track 63. Listen. Write the types of transportation. Use the words in the box.

> drive   take a taxi   ~~take the bus~~   take the train

1. **A:** Where are you going?

    B: I'm going to English class.

    A: Oh. How do you get to school?

    B: I _____ *take the bus* _____.

2. **A:** Where are you going?

    B: I'm going to work.

    A: Oh. How do you get to work?

    B: I _____.

3. **A:** Where are you going?

    B: I'm going to the library.

    A: Oh. How do you get to the library?

    B: I _____.

4. **A:** Where are you going?

    B: I'm going to the supermarket.

    A: Oh. How do you get to the supermarket?

    B: I _____.

C Write about yourself. Answer the questions.

1. How do you get to school? _____

2. How do you get to work? _____

3. How do you get to the library? _____

4. How do you get to the supermarket? _____

A Look at the arrows. Write the directions. Use the words in the box.

> Go straight.   ~~Turn left~~.   Turn right.

1. ___Turn left.___

2. _____

3. _____

B Play Track 64. Listen. Write the missing words.

1. **A:** Excuse me. Where is the train station?

   B: It's on First Avenue. ___Go___ ___straight___ for one block.

   Then _____ _____ on First Avenue.

   A: Thanks a lot!

2. **A:** Excuse me. Where is the supermarket?

   B: It's on Second Avenue. _____ _____ on Main Street.

   Then _____ _____ for one block.

   A: Thanks a lot!

3. **A:** Excuse me. Where is the bank?

   B: It's on Third Avenue. _____ _____ on Central Street.

   Then _____ _____ on Third Avenue.

   A: Thanks a lot!

C Look at the maps. Read the directions. Write the places.

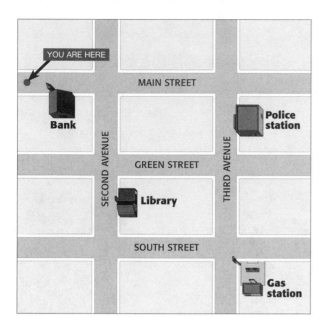

1. Go straight for two blocks.

   Then turn right on Third Avenue.

   police station

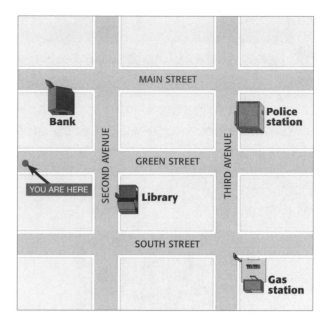

2. Go straight for one block.

   Then turn right on Second Avenue.

   _____

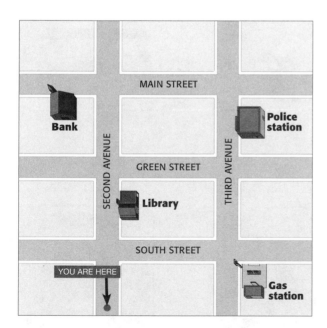

3. Go straight for three blocks.

   Then turn left on Main Street.

   _____

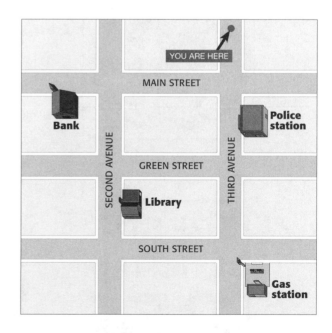

4. Go straight for three blocks.

   Then turn left on South Street.

   _____

A Look at the pictures. Write the words. Use the words in the box.

> no left turn no U-turn speed limit 25 miles per hour train crossing yield
> no parking one-way street stop sign ~~walk/don't walk~~

1. <u>walk / don't walk</u> 2. _____ 3. _____

4. _____ 5. _____ 6. _____

7. _____ 8. _____ 9. _____

B Look at the pictures. Circle *Yes* or *No.*

1.  Do you stop?   Yes   (No)

2.  Do you walk?   Yes   No

3.  Do you stop?   Yes   No

4.  Do you park here?   Yes   No

5.  Do you go one way only?   Yes   No

6.  Do you turn left?   Yes   No

7. Do you yield?   Yes   No

8.  Do you make a U-turn?   Yes   No

Lesson 6: Hong's story

A 🔘 Play Track 65. Listen to the story.
Number the sentences in the correct order.

_____ I need to show the bank my business plan.

_____ I have a dream.

_1_ My name is Hong.

_____ I want to open my own restaurant here.

_____ I need to go to City Hall for a business license.

_____ In my country, I worked in a restaurant.

_____ Here in the United States, I'm a cook, too.

_____ Soon my family and friends can eat at my new restaurant!

_____ I need to go to the bank for a loan.

_____ I was a cook.

B Read the sentences in Exercise A again. Write the story.

My name is Hong. _____

_____

_____

_____

_____

_____

C 🔘 Play Track 65 again to check your answers to Exercise B.

A Look at the pictures. Write *a* or *i*.

1. b__i__ke

2. l____brary

3. t____xi

4. b____nk

5. s____gn

6. g____s station

B Play Track 66 to check your answers to Exercise A.

C Play Track 67. Listen. Write the words.

1. _____bike_____

6. _____

2. _____

7. _____

3. _____

8. _____

4. _____

9. _____

5. _____

10. _____

Unit 11: Get well soon!

Lesson 1: The body • Make an appointment

A Look at the picture. Write the parts of the body. Use the words in the box.

> arm   ~~ear~~   foot   knee   neck   shoulder
> chest   eye   hand   leg   nose   stomach

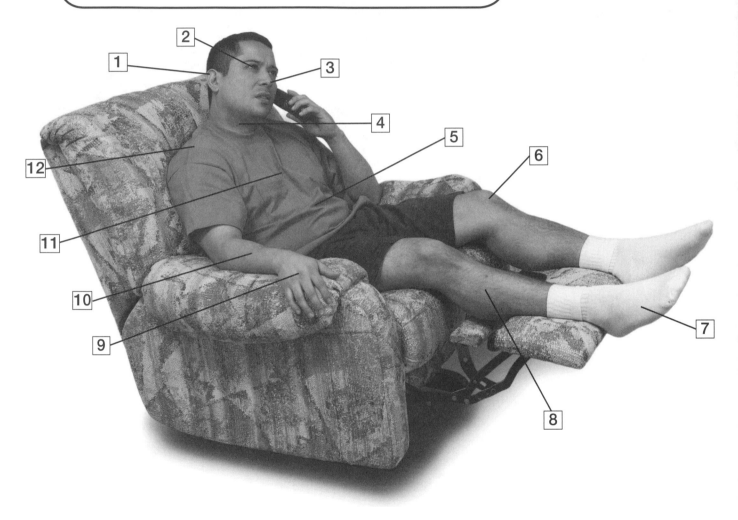

1. _____ear_____   5. _____   9. _____

2. _____   6. _____   10. _____

3. _____   7. _____   11. _____

4. _____   8. _____   12. _____

B 🔘 **Play Track 68. Listen for the part of the body. Circle *a* or *b*.**

1. (a.) stomach   b. shoulder
2. a. hand   b. arm
3. a. foot   b. feet
4. a. ear   b. eye
5. a. feet   b. knee
6. a. chest   b. leg
7. a. neck   b. nose
8. a. hand   b. arm

C **Look at the pictures. Complete the sentences.**

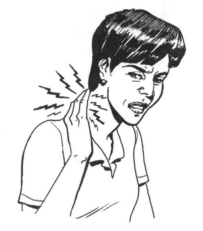

1. Her _____ neck hurts _____.

2. His _____.

3. Her _____.

4. His _____.

Ⓐ Look at the pictures. Complete the medical instructions.
Use the words in the box.

~~Breathe~~   jacket   Lie   mouth   out   sleeves   Step   straight   table

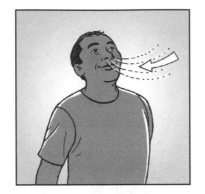

1. _Breathe_ in.

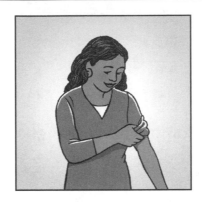

2. Roll up your _____.

3. Look _____ ahead.

4. _____ down.

5. Take off your _____.

6. Open your _____.

7. Breathe _____.

8. _____ on the scale.

9. Sit on the _____.

B  Play Track 69. Listen to the instructions.
Match the instructions with the pictures.

a. ____

b. _1_

c. ____

d. ____

C Read the story.

Joe gets a checkup every year. He has an appointment on Thursday. He goes to the health clinic. The doctor checks him. Joe follows the doctor's instructions. The doctor says, "You are in good health."

D Read the story again.
Check (✓) the correct sentences.

☑ 1. Joe gets a checkup every year.

☐ 2. Joe has a doctor's appointment on Tuesday.

☐ 3. His appointment is at the health clinic.

☐ 4. Joe gives the doctor instructions.

☐ 5. Joe is in good health.

A Match the pictures with the words.

a.

b.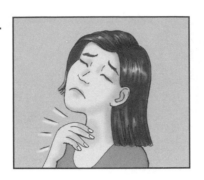

c.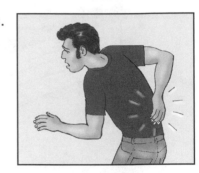

d.

e.

f.

g.

h.

i.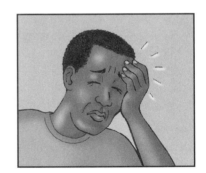

1. the flu __f__

2. a stomachache ____

3. a cough ____

4. a fever ____

5. a headache ____

6. a sore throat ____

7. a backache ____

8. a cold ____

9. a toothache ____

B Look at the pictures. Write the correct suggestions from the box.

> drink a lot of liquids   get a lot of rest   stay home from work   ~~take an aspirin~~

1.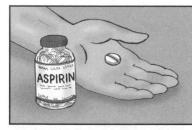

   A: What's the matter?

   B: I have a headache.

   A: You should _____ *take an aspirin* _____.

2.

   A: What's the matter?

   B: I have a cold.

   A: You should _____.

3.

   A: What's the matter?

   B: I have a fever.

   A: You should _____.

4.

   A: What's the matter?

   B: I have the flu.

   A: You should _____.

C Write suggestions. Use *should.*

1. (take an aspirin) *You should take an aspirin.* _____

2. (stay home from school) _____

3. (stay home from work) _____

4. (drink a lot of liquids) _____

A Look at the pictures. Write sentences. Use the sentences in the box.

> My friend is having a heart attack.   There is a building on fire.
> ~~Someone robbed my house.~~   There was a car accident.

1. _Someone robbed my house._   2. _____

_____   _____

3. _____   4. _____

_____   _____

B Play Track 70. Listen. Choose the correct sentence. Circle *a* or *b.*

1. (a.) Someone robbed the woman's house.   b. The woman is having a heart attack.

2. a. The woman is on Main Street.   b. The woman is on Oak Street.

3. a. The woman is in Oak City.   b. The woman is in Lake City.

4. a. The cross street is Main Street.   b. The cross street is Oak Street.

C 💿 **Play Track 71. Listen. Write the missing words and numbers.**

1. **A:** 911. What's your emergency?

   B: There is a building on _____ *fire* _____.

   A: Where are you?

   B: _____ *1402* _____ Oak Avenue in Park City.

   A: What's the cross street?

   B: Third Street.

2. **A:** 911. What's your emergency?

   B: My friend is having a _____ attack.

   A: Where are you?

   B: _____ Park Avenue in River City.

   A: What's the cross street?

   B: First Street.

3. **A:** 911. What's your emergency?

   B: Someone _____ my house.

   A: Where are you?

   B: _____ Third Avenue in Maple City.

   A: What's the cross street?

   B: Main Street.

4. **A:** 911. What's your emergency?

   B: There was a _____ accident.

   A: Where are you?

   B: _____ Fourth Avenue in Green City.

   A: What's the cross street?

   B: Lake Street.

A Look at the pictures. Circle *a* or *b*.

1. a. cough syrup
    b. aspirin

2. a. 1 teaspoon
    b. 2 teaspoons

3. a. every 4 hours
    b. twice a day

4. a. capsules
    b. tablets

5. a. every 4 hours
    b. twice a day

6. a. cough syrup
    b. prescription medicine

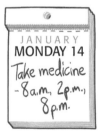

7. a. every 6 hours
    b. every 4 hours

8. a. tablets
    b. capsules

9. a. prescription medicine
    b. cough syrup

B 💿 Play Track 72. Listen. Read the sentences. Circle *Yes* or *No*.

1. Miguel doesn't feel well.   Yes   No

2. He has a fever and a headache.   Yes   No

3. He is taking prescription medicine.   Yes   No

4. The directions say take 2 tablets twice a day.   Yes   No

5. The directions say take the medicine with food. Yes   No

C Read the directions on the label.

D Read the directions on the label again. Answer the questions.
Use the words in the box.

> 1 tablet   6 hours   aspirin   doctor   ~~pain and fever~~   water

1. The medicine is for __pain and fever__ .

2. Sara has a headache and a fever. She should take some _____.

3. Sara is 32 years old. She should take _____.

4. Sara should take the medicine every _____.

5. Sara should take the medicine with _____.

6. After six days, Sara still has a fever. She should see a _____.

A 🔘 Play Track 73. Listen to the story.
Number the sentences in the correct order.

_____ My daughter is 23 years old.

_____ But I feel healthy.

_1_ My name is Mariam.

_____ I'm 45 years old.

_____ Why should I go to a doctor?

_____ I don't feel sick.

_____ Now my family and I are in the United States.

_____ She says it's important.

_____ She says that women here have a checkup every year.

_____ In my country, people go to the doctor when they are sick.

B Read the sentences in Exercise A again. Write the story.

My name is Mariam.

_____

_____

_____

_____

_____

_____

C 🔘 Play Track 73 again to check your answers to Exercise B.

A Play Track 74. Listen. Write e or i.

1. s___i___ck

2. sl____ ____p

3. s____t

4. s____ ____

5. str____ ____t

6. dr____nk

7. h____s

8. w____ ____k

9. f____ ____l

10. s____nk

11. kn____ ____

12. l ____sten

B Play Track 75. Listen. Write the words.

1. _____ sick _____

2. _____

3. _____

4. _____

5. _____

6. _____

7. _____

8. _____

9. _____

10. _____

Unit 12: What do you do?

Lesson 1: Jobs

A Match the pictures with the words.

a.

b.

c.

d.

e.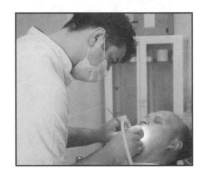

f.

g.

h.

i.

1. a homemaker _f_

2. a teacher's assistant ____

3. a housekeeper ____

4. a painter ____

5. a bus driver ____

6. a sales assistant ____

7. a mechanic ____

8. a dentist ____

9. a construction worker ____

B Look at the pictures. Write the jobs. Use the words in the box.

> a bus driver   a dentist   a housekeeper   ~~a mechanic~~
>
> a construction worker   a homemaker   a painter   a sales assistant

1.

A: I'm _____*a mechanic*_____.

What do you do?

B: I'm _____.

2.

A: I'm _____.

What do you do?

B: I'm _____.

3.

A: I'm _____.

What do you do?

B: I'm _____.

4.

A: I'm _____.

What do you do?

B: I'm _____.

A Look at the pictures. Write the jobs. Use the words in the box.

> a cashier ~~a custodian~~ a factory worker an office assistant a waiter
> a cook a doctor a nurse a security guard

1. _____a custodian_____

2. _____

3. _____

4. _____

5. _____

6. _____

7. _____

8. _____

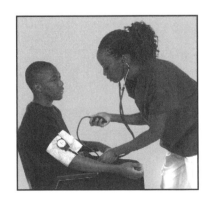

9. _____

B Write *do* or *does*.

1. Where _____*does*_____ he work?

2. Where _____ they work?

3. Where _____ she work?

4. Where _____ you work?

5. Where _____ Maria work?

6. Where _____ Tom work?

7. Where _____ Sun-Li and Ann work?

8. Where _____ Bill and Chad work?

C Write questions. Use the words in parentheses and *Where do* or *Where does*.

1. (you / work) _Where do you work?_____

2. (Nancy / work) _____

3. (they / work) _____

4. (Rafal / work) _____

5. (Tien and Monika / work) _____

6. (she / work) _____

D Answer the questions. Use true or made-up information.

1. Where do you work? _____

2. Where does your teacher work? _____

3. Where does your doctor work? _____

4. Where does your friend work? _____

A Look at the pictures. Write the job skills. Use the words in the box.

build houses	help customers	use a cash register
drive a truck	help sick people	use a computer
~~fix cars~~	speak two languages	use office machines

1. _fix cars_

2. _____

3. _____

4. _____

5. _____

6. _____

7. _____

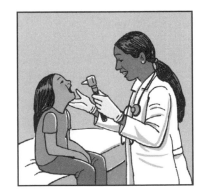

8. _____

9. _____

B Write the job skills. Use the words in the box.

> build houses ~~help customers~~ use a cash register
> fix cars help sick people use office machines

1. **A:** What are your job skills?

   B: I'm a sales assistant.

   I _help customers_____.

   And I can use a cash register.

2. **A:** What are your job skills?

   B: I'm a construction worker.

   I _____.

   And I can speak two languages.

3. **A:** What are your job skills?

   B: I'm a mechanic. I _____.

   And I help customers.

4. **A:** What are your job skills?

   B: I'm a doctor. I _____.

   And I speak three languages.

5. **A:** What are your job skills?

   B: I'm a cashier. I _____.

   And I help customers.

6. **A:** What are your job skills?

   B: I'm an office assistant. I _____.

   And I use a computer.

A Complete the sentences. Use *I*, *he*, *she,* or *they* and *can* or *can't*.

1. Can you fix cars?   Yes, _____*I can*_____.

2. Can he use a computer?   No, _____.

3. Can she help customers?   No, _____.

4. Can they speak two languages?   Yes, _____.

5. Can he drive a truck?   Yes, _____.

B Look at the pictures. Complete the questions. Write true answers.

1. **A:** Can you _____*use a computer*_____?

   B: _____.

2. **A:** Can you _____?

   B: _____.

3. **A:** Can you _____?

   B: _____.

4. **A:** Can you _____?

   B: _____.

C Write the questions and answers.

1. (can / Mrs. Smith / speak two languages)

    A: _Can Mrs. Smith speak two languages_ ?

    B: Yes, _____ she can _____.

2. (can / Mr. Lim / use a computer)

    A: _____?

    B: No, _____.

3. (can / Ms. Popova / fix cars)

    A: _____?

    B: Yes, _____.

4. (can / you / build houses)

    A: _____?

    B: No, _____.

5. (can / Eric and Katrina / use a cash register)

    A: _____?

    B: Yes, _____.

6. (can / you / help customers)

    A: _____?

    B: No, _____.

7. (can / Mr. Nowak / use office machines)

    A: _____?

    B: Yes, _____.

8. (can / Alex and Marie / drive a truck)

    A: _____?

    B: No, _____.

A Read the job ad.

> **Help Wanted**
> Ed's Department Store
> PT sales assistant
> Wknds
> Call 659-555-8841 for interview appointment

B Read the job ad again. Circle *Yes* or *No.*

1. The job is full-time.	Yes	(No)
2. The job is for a sales assistant.	Yes	No
3. Experience is required.	Yes	No
4. You need to work Saturday and Sunday.	Yes	No
5. You need to call for an interview appointment.	Yes	No

C Read the ads.

> **Help Wanted**
> MKA Factory
> PT factory worker
> Exp req
> Wknds
> Apply in person

A

> **Help Wanted**
> City Supermarket
> Cashier
> FT M–F
> Call 459-555-9321 for
> interview appointment

B

D Read the ads in Exercise C again. Match the sentences with the ads. Circle *A* or *B*.

1. The job is for a factory worker.   Ⓐ   B
2. The job is full-time.   A   B
3. The job is part-time.   A   B
4. You need experience.   A   B
5. You need to work on weekends.   A   B
6. You need to work Monday to Friday.   A   B
7. You need to call for an interview.   A   B
8. You need to apply in person.   A   B

E Match the sentences.

1. I work 12 hours a week. __d__   a. I work full-time.
2. I need to have experience. ____   b. I have to go in person.
3. I was a housekeeper in my country. ____   c. I work weekends.
4. I have to go to the office for my interview. ____   d. I work part-time.
5. I work 40 hours a week. ____   e. Experience is required.
6. I work Saturdays and Sundays. ____   f. I have experience as a housekeeper.

F Circle *Yes* or *No* about yourself.

1. I work full-time.   Yes   No
2. I work part-time.   Yes   No
3. I have experience as a cook.   Yes   No
4. I have experience as a housekeeper.   Yes   No
5. I work weekends.   Yes   No
6. I work Monday to Friday.   Yes   No

A ◎ Play Track 76. Listen to the story.
Number the sentences in the correct order.

_____ I need to get to the interview early.

_1_ My name is Monika.

_____ I need to remember three important things.

_____ I need to make eye contact.

_____ Wish me luck!

_____ I feel confident.

_____ I need to remember to shake hands firmly.

_____ I practiced my interview skills in my English class.

_____ I have my first job interview in the United States on Thursday.

B Read the sentences in Exercise A again. Write the story.

My name is Monika. _____

_____

_____

_____

_____

_____

_____

C ◎ Play Track 76 again to check your answers to Exercise B.

A Look at the pictures. Write *o* or *u*.

1. d_*o*_ctor

2. b____s

3. c____stodian

4. d____llar

5. h____spital

6. dr____gstore

B Play Track 77 to check your answers to Exercise A.

C Play Track 78. Listen. Write the words.

1. _____*doctor*_____   6. _____

2. _____   7. _____

3. _____   8. _____

4. _____   9. _____

5. _____   10. _____

Audio Script

UNIT 1

Page 4, Exercise C

1. A: What's your name, please?
   B: My name is Hong Chen.
   A: Spell your first name.
   B: H-O-N-G.
   A: Spell your last name.
   B: C-H-E-N.
2. A: What's your name, please?
   B: Anna Novak.
   A: Spell your first name.
   B: A-N-N-A.
   A: Spell your last name.
   B: N-O-V-A-K.
3. A: What's your name, please?
   B: My name is Mark Smith.
   A: Spell your first name.
   B: M-A-R-K.
   A: Spell your last name.
   B: S-M-I-T-H.
4. A: What's your name, please?
   B: My name is Carla Diaz.
   A: Spell your first name.
   B: C-A-R-L-A.
   A: Spell your last name.
   B: D-I-A-Z.

Page 5, Exercise B

1. A: What's your student ID number?
   B: 53691.
   A: 53691?
   B: That's right.
2. A: What's your student ID number?
   B: 02469.
   A: 02469?
   B: That's right.
3. A: What's your student ID number?
   B: 26750.
   A: 26750?
   B: That's right.
4. A: What's your student ID number?
   B: 63980.
   A: 63980?
   B: That's right.

Page 5, Exercise C

1. A: What's your phone number?
   B: 674-555-5831.
2. A: What's your phone number?
   B: 829-555-1194.
3. A: What's your phone number?
   B: 427-555-6850.
4. A: What's your phone number?
   B: 350-555-7448.
5. A: What's your phone number?
   B: 914-555-8132.
6. A: What's your phone number?
   B: 201-555-4990.

Page 8, Exercise C

1. She's the teacher.
2. He's from Canada.
3. She's my friend.
4. She's a good teacher.
5. He's a new student.
6. She's from El Salvador.
7. He's a good student.
8. He's from Korea.

Page 10, Exercise B

1. They're from Somalia.
2. We're from the United States.
3. They're in the classroom.
4. You're a good student.
5. We're new students.
6. You're my classmate.

Page 12, Exercises A and C

My name is Ivan. I'm a student.
I say hello to a classmate and I smile.
In my school, some students say hello and shake hands.
Some students say hello and hug.
Some students say hello and bow.
Other students say hello and kiss.
How do you say hello?

Page 13, Exercise A

1. map
2. phone
3. my
4. China
5. Mexico
6. number
7. classroom
8. students
9. nice
10. from
11. listen
12. meet

Page 13, Exercise B

1. map
2. answer
3. number
4. my
5. welcome
6. friend
7. students
8. listen
9. nice
10. phone

UNIT 2

Page 15, Exercise B

1. Do you have a notebook?
2. Do you have a backpack?
3. Do you have a pen?
4. Do you have a cell phone?
5. Do you have a dictionary?

Page 19, Exercise B

1. A: Where is Mr. Lee?
   B: He's in the library.
2. A: Where is Carol?
   B: She's in the cafeteria.
3. A: Where is your teacher?
   B: He's in the classroom.
4. A: Where is your classmate?
   B: She's in the bookstore.
5. A: Where is your book?
   B: It's in the computer lab.
6. A: Where is Yolanda?
   B: She's in the office.

Page 23, Exercise B

A: How do you study English?
B: I go to class, and I ask the teacher questions.
A: That's great!
B: How do you study English?
A: I practice with my classmates. At home, I write in my notebook.

Page 24, Exercises A and C

My name is Lan.
In my country, students don't talk in class.
They listen to the teacher.
In the United States, students talk in groups.
In my class, students ask many questions.
My teacher listens to the students.

Page 25, Exercise B

1. pen
2. notebook
3. pencil
4. book
5. piece of paper
6. backpack

Page 25, Exercise C

1. pen
2. practice
3. library
4. paper
5. number
6. open
7. birth
8. backpack
9. book
10. notebook

UNIT 3

Page 26, Exercise A

1. nine
2. fifteen
3. twenty-three
4. thirty-six
5. forty
6. fifty-two

Page 28, Exercise B

1. A: What time is your English class?
   B: It's at 9:15.
2. A: What time is your break?
   B: It's at 10:40.
3. A: What time is your computer class?
   B: It's at 12:30.
4. A: What time is your break?
   B: It's at 2:45.

Page 28, Exercise C

1. A: What time is your English class?
   B: It's from 9:15 to 1:15.
2. A: What time is your break?
   B: It's from 11:15 to 11:45.
3. A: What time is your math class?
   B: It's from 12:30 to 2.
4. A: What time is your break?
   B: It's from 2 to 2:20.

Page 31, Exercise D

1. He goes to work at 7:45.
2. She gets dressed at 8:15.
3. He goes to school at 9:00.
4. She eats breakfast at 6:00.
5. He gets home at 5:30.

Page 32, Exercise B

1. He goes to work at 7:00 on Monday.
2. She goes to school at 5:00 on Wednesday.
3. He gets up at 9:30 on Saturday.
4. She goes to sleep at 10:30 on Tuesday.
5. She goes to the library at 9:00 on Sunday.

Page 35, Exercise E

1. five fifteen
2. six oh eight
3. four twelve
4. two thirty

Page 35, Exercise F

1. ninety-three
2. eighty
3. seventeen
4. thirteen
5. twenty
6. seventy-nine
7. one hundred
8. forty-four

Page 36, Exercises A and C

Carlo likes to be on time.
He gets up early and gets ready for work.
He gets to work at 6:50. He starts work at 7:00.
Carlo goes to school after work.
He is always early for class.
On weekends, Carlo meets friends. He is always late!

Page 37, Exercise A

1. dinner
2. twenty
3. time
4. don't
5. fifteen
6. two
7. Thursday
8. Sunday
9. Monday
10. get dressed
11. eat breakfast
12. twenty-two

Page 37, Exercise B

1. dinner
2. time
3. do
4. twelve
5. ten
6. does
7. get
8. read
9. day
10. breakfast

UNIT 4

Page 39, Exercise B

1. A: Who's that?
   B: That's my father.
2. A: Who's that?
   B: That's my wife.

3. A: Who's that?
   B: That's my husband.
4. A: Who's that?
   B: That's my brother.
5. A: Who's that?
   B: That's my mother.
6. A: Who's that?
   B: That's my daughter.
7. A: Who's that?
   B: That's my grandfather.
8. A: Who's that?
   B: That's my sister.
9. A: Who's that?
   B: That's my grandmother.
10. A: Who's that?
    B: That's my son.

Page 44, Exercise B

1. A: When is your birthday?
   B: December second.
2. A: When is your birthday?
   B: March seventh.
3. A: When is your birthday?
   B: July fifth.
4. A: When is your birthday?
   B: August eighteenth.
5. A: When is your birthday?
   B: October twenty-second.
6. A: When is your birthday?
   B: June thirtieth.

Page 48, Exercises A and C

Ernesto and Maria are married.
In their country, men go to work.
In their country, women stay at home. They do all the
     household chores.
In the United States, both Maria and Ernesto go to work.
Ernesto helps at home. He does the dishes.
Sometimes Ernesto goes to the supermarket, too.

Page 49, Exercise A

1. dishes
2. third
3. date
4. mother
5. husband
6. daughter
7. there
8. laundry
9. brother
10. grandfather
11. thirteenth
12. grandmother

Page 49, Exercise B

1. dishes	6. month
2. the	7. father
3. they	8. December
4. laundry	9. date
5. that	10. there

UNIT 5

Page 53, Exercise C

1. A: Do you have change for a five?
   B: Yes. I have five singles.
2. A: Do you have change for a fifty?
   B: Yes. I have a twenty and three tens.
3. A: Do you have change for a ten?
   B: Yes. I have a five and five singles.
4. A: Do you have change for a hundred?
   B: Yes. I have a fifty, a twenty, and three tens.

Page 57, Exercise B

1. twenty-two cents
2. seventy-eight cents
3. sixty-four cents
4. sixteen cents
5. forty-three cents
6. ninety-seven cents

Page 57, Exercise C

1. a dollar fifty-nine
2. eighty-six forty-nine
3. seven twenty-eight
4. fifty-nine sixty-three
5. ninety-five forty
6. thirty-two fifteen

Page 57, Exercise D

1. A: Excuse me. How much is soap?
   B: A dollar seventy-five.
2. A: Excuse me. How much are batteries?
   B: Four seventy-eight.
3. A: Excuse me. How much is aspirin?
   B: Six twenty-nine.
4. A: Excuse me. How much are tissues?
   B: A dollar sixty.
5. A: Excuse me. How much is deodorant?
   B: Three fifteen.
6. A: Excuse me. How much is toilet paper?
   B: Two twenty.

Page 60, Exercises A and C

My name is Edna. In my country, I shop at markets.
I talk to the salespeople about the prices.
I get good bargains.
In the United States, I shop in big stores.
I pay the price on the price tag.
How do I get good bargains? I buy things on sale!

Page 61, Exercise A

1. go	7. price tag
2. shaving cream	8. count
3. big	9. good
4. country	10. drugstore
5. get	11. cash
6. computer	12. coin

Page 61, Exercise B

1. go	6. big
2. cash	7. price tag
3. computer	8. drugstore
4. good	9. coin
5. count	10. get

UNIT 6

Page 63, Exercise B

1. A: Do we need vegetables?
   B: Yes. Get tomatoes and onions.
2. A: Do we need vegetables?
   B: Yes. Get peppers and mushrooms.
3. A: Do we need vegetables?
   B: Yes. Get cucumbers and lettuce.
4. A: Do we need vegetables?
   B: Yes. Get potatoes and peppers.
5. A: Do we need vegetables?
   B: Yes. Get carrots and onions.
6. A: Do we need vegetables?
   B: Yes. Get tomatoes and peppers.

Page 65, Exercise B

1. A: Do you like vegetables?
   B: I like peas. I don't like onions.
2. A: Do you like vegetables?
   B: I like potatoes. I don't like peppers.
3. A: Do you like vegetables?
   B: I like tomatoes. I don't like mushrooms.
4. A: Do you like vegetables?
   B: I like cucumbers. I don't like carrots.

Page 71, Exercise B

1. A: Are you ready to order?
   B: I'd like a chicken sandwich, French fries, and milk.
2. A: Are you ready to order?
   B: I'd like a hamburger, a green salad, and iced tea.
3. A: Are you ready to order?
   B: I'd like a taco, a baked potato, and ice cream.
4. A: Are you ready to order?
   B: I'd like a fish sandwich, rice, and coffee.
5. A: Are you ready to order?
   B: I'd like a taco, a fruit salad, and iced tea.

Page 72, Exercises A and C

My name is Tran. In my country, people usually eat
   with chopsticks.
Sometimes children eat with their fingers.
My name is Kyoko. In my country, people usually drink
   their soup.
In the United States, people usually eat with forks, knives,
   and spoons.
Sometimes they eat food with their fingers, like sandwiches
   and French fries.
How do you eat in your country?

Page 73, Exercise A

1.	fruit	7.	beef
2.	vegetables	8.	coffee
3.	very	9.	live
4.	food	10.	fifteen
5.	fish	11.	five
6.	have	12.	favorite

Page 73, Exercise B

1.	fruit	6.	fish
2.	vegetables	7.	have
3.	Friday	8.	five
4.	food	9.	favorite
5.	live	10.	beef

UNIT 7

Page 76, Exercise B

1. A: Can you tell me about the apartment for rent?
   B: There is a sunny living room and a small kitchen.
   A: It sounds nice.
2. A: Can you tell me about the apartment for rent?
   B: There is a large garage and a sunny dining room.
   A: It sounds nice.
3. A: Can you tell me about the apartment for rent?
   B: There is a large closet and a small basement.
   A: It sounds nice.
4. A: Can you tell me about the apartment for rent?
   B: There is a sunny bedroom and a modern kitchen.
   A: It sounds nice.
5. A: Can you tell me about the apartment for rent?
   B: There is a large kitchen and a modern bathroom.
   A: It sounds nice.

Page 79, Exercise C

1. A: Is there a stove in the apartment?
   B: Yes, there is.
2. A: Are there any lamps in the apartment?
   B: No, there aren't.
3. A: Are there any chairs in the apartment?
   B: Yes, there are.
4. A: Is there a washing machine in the apartment?
   B: No, there isn't.
5. A: Are there any tables in the apartment?
   B: No, there aren't.
6. A: Is there a bed in the apartment?
   B: Yes, there is.

Page 81, Exercise C

1. 13 Martin Street
2. 50 Angelo Drive
3. 167 Green Boulevard
4. 20 South Lane
5. 184 Meadow Road
6. 1245 Erie Avenue

Page 84, Exercises A and C

   Alicia is 21 years old. She is single. Alicia lives with her
older sister and her brother-in-law in California. Alicia has a
good job. Now she wants to move to an apartment with her
friends. But Alicia's parents are not happy. In their country,
single people live with their families. In the United States,
single people often live alone or with friends. What should
Alicia do?

Page 85, Exercise B

1.	dishwasher	4.	chair
2.	dresser	5.	refrigerator
3.	table	6.	lamp

Page 85, Exercise C

1. dishwasher
2. large
3. room
4. lamp
5. address
6. closet
7. boulevard
8. road
9. living room
10. refrigerator

UNIT 8

Page 87, Exercise B

1. I need a new shirt.
2. I need a new skirt.
3. I need a new T-shirt.
4. I need new sneakers.
5. I need new jeans.
6. I need a new dress.

Page 87, Exercise C

1. A: Let's go shopping! I need a new jacket.
   B: OK. I need shoes.
2. A: Let's go shopping! I need new pants.
   B: OK. I need a blouse.
3. A: Let's go shopping! I need a new sweater.
   B: OK. I need a shirt.
4. A: Let's go shopping. I need new sneakers.
   B: OK. I need jeans.

Page 88, Exercise A

1. A: Can I help you?
   B: Do you have this shirt in a large?
   A: Yes. Here you go.
   B: Do you have these sneakers in a size 11?
   A: I'm sorry. We don't.
2. A: Can I help you?
   B: Do you have this blouse in a medium?
   A: Yes. Here you go.
   B: Do you have these jeans in a size 10?
   A: I'm sorry. We don't.
3. A: Can I help you?
   B: Do you have this T-shirt in an extra large?
   A: Yes. Here you go.
   B: Do you have these shoes in a size 12?
   A: I'm sorry. We don't.

Page 90, Exercise C

1. Monika is wearing a black jacket.
2. Meg is wearing a red skirt.
3. Jin-Su is wearing a blue shirt.
4. Dora is wearing beige pants.
5. Solomon is wearing white shoes.
6. Li is wearing a purple sweater.
7. Miguel is wearing gray socks.
8. Anne is wearing a blue dress.

Page 93, Exercise D

A: I need to return a sweater and some sneakers.
B: What's the problem?
A: The sweater is too long and the sneakers are too big. Here's my receipt.

Page 95, Exercise C

1. A: What store is having a sale?
   B: Clara's Store is having a sale.
2. A: When is the sale?
   B: The sale is on Thursday.
3. A: What time does the store open?
   B: The store opens at 9:00.
4. A: How much are the jackets?
   B: The jackets are $15.50.
5. A: How much are the shoes?
   B: The shoes are $25.00.
6. A: How much are the shirts?
   B: The shirts are $19.99.

Page 96, Exercises A and C

My name is Yun. My wedding is in August. I want to wear a long white dress. In my country, people wear white for funerals. Women wear a red and green dress on their wedding day. My mother and grandmother want me to wear a red and green dress. What should I do?

Page 97, Exercise B

1. skirt
2. shirt
3. shoes
4. sweater
5. pants
6. T-shirt

Page 97, Exercise C

1. skirt
2. she
3. small
4. shopping
5. T-shirt
6. short
7. size
8. sale
9. suit
10. should

UNIT 9

Page 107, Exercise C

1. A: Hello?
   B: Hi. This is Marisa Costas. Can I speak to Mr. Clark?
   A: Mr. Clark is taking a break now. Can I take a message?
   B: Please tell him I'm not coming to work today.
   A: OK. What's your phone number?
   B: It's 212-555-6798.
2. A: Hello?
   B: Hi. This is Ann. Can I speak to Kyoko?
   A: Kyoko is not here. Can I take a message?
   B: Please tell her I'm not going to the movies today.
   A: OK. What's your phone number?
   B: It's 512-555-9841.
3. A: Hello?
   B: Hi. This is Sam White. Can I speak to Ms. Popova?
   A: Ms. Popova is out of the office. Can I take a message?
   B: Please tell her I'm not coming to class today.
   A: OK. What's your phone number?
   B: It's 479-555-8310.

Page 108, Exercises A and C

My name is Alfonso. I have two children. They are busy every weekend with their friends. They talk on the phone and go shopping. They play sports and watch TV. On weekends, my wife and I eat alone. Our children don't sit down with us to eat. In my country, families eat together on weekends. Then they spend time relaxing and talking. What do you do on weekends? Do you spend time with your family or friends?

Page 109, Exercise A

1. message
2. date
3. help
4. take
5. name
6. every
7. today
8. hello
9. exercise
10. newspaper
11. Wednesday
12. sentence

Page 109, Exercise B

1. message
2. yes
3. play
4. name
5. today
6. sentence
7. make
8. spend
9. later
10. help

UNIT 10

Page 115, Exercise B

1. A: Where are you going?
   B: I'm going to English class.
   A: Oh. How do you get to school?
   B: I take the bus.
2. A: Where are you going?
   B: I'm going to work.
   A: Oh. How do you get to work?
   B: I take the train.
3. A: Where are you going?
   B: I'm going to the library.
   A: Oh. How do you get to the library?
   B: I take a taxi.
4. A: Where are you going?
   B: I'm going to the supermarket.
   A: Oh. How do you get to the supermarket?
   B: I drive.

Page 116, Exercise B

1. A: Excuse me. Where is the train station?
   B: It's on First Avenue. Go straight for one block. Then turn right on First Avenue.
   A: Thanks a lot!
2. A: Excuse me. Where is the supermarket?
   B: It's on Second Avenue. Turn left on Main Street. Then go straight for one block.
   A: Thanks a lot!
3. A: Excuse me. Where is the bank?
   B: It's on Third Avenue. Turn right on Central Street. Then turn left on Third Avenue.
   A: Thanks a lot!

Page 120, Exercises A and C

My name is Hong. In my country, I worked in a restaurant. I was a cook. Here in the United States, I'm a cook, too. I have a dream. I want to open my own restaurant here. I need to go to City Hall for a business license. I need to go to the bank for a loan. I need to show the bank my business plan. Soon my family and friends can eat at my new restaurant!

Page 121, Exercise B

1. bike
2. library
3. taxi
4. bank
5. sign
6. gas station

Page 121, Exercise C

1.	bike	6.	thanks
2.	answer	7.	family
3.	ride	8.	license
4.	gas	9.	write
5.	drive	10.	sign

UNIT 11

Page 123, Exercise B

1. A: What's the problem?
   B: My stomach hurts.
2. A: What's the problem?
   B: My arm hurts.
3. A: What's the problem?
   B: My foot hurts.
4. A: What's the problem?
   B: My ear hurts.
5. A: What's the problem?
   B: My knee hurts.
6. A: What's the problem?
   B: My leg hurts.
7. A: What's the problem?
   B: My neck hurts.
8. A: What's the problem?
   B: My hand hurts.

Page 125, Exercise B

1. Take off your jacket.
2. Sit on the table.
3. Lie down.
4. Step on the scale.

Page 128, Exercise B

A: 911. What's your emergency?
B: Someone robbed my house.
A: Where are you?
B: 15 Main Street in Lake City.
A: What's the cross street?
B: Oak Street.

Page 129, Exercise C

1. A: 911. What's your emergency?
   B: There is a building on fire.
   A: Where are you?
   B: 1402 Oak Avenue in Park City.
   A: What's the cross street?
   B: Third Street.
2. A: 911. What's your emergency?
   B: My friend is having a heart attack.
   A: Where are you?
   B: 8756 Park Avenue in River City.
   A: What's the cross street?
   B: First Street.
3. A: 911. What's your emergency?
   B: Someone robbed my house.
   A: Where are you?
   B: 4739 Third Avenue in Maple City.
   A: What's the cross street?
   B: Main Street.
4. A: 911. What's your emergency?
   B: There was a car accident.
   A: Where are you?
   B: 3289 Fourth Avenue in Green City.
   A: What's the cross street?
   B: Lake Street.

Page 130, Exercise B

A: Hi, Miguel. How are you?
B: I don't feel well. I have a fever and an ear infection.
A: Oh, that's too bad. Are you taking medicine?
B: Yes. I'm taking prescription medicine.
A: That's good. How often do you take it?
B: I have to take 2 tablets twice a day with water.
A: I hope you feel better soon!

Page 132, Exercises A and C

My name is Mariam. I'm 45 years old. In my country, people go to the doctor when they are sick. Now my family and I are in the United States. My daughter is 23 years old. She says that women here have a checkup every year. She says it's important. But I feel healthy. I don't feel sick. Why should I go to a doctor?

Page 133, Exercise A

1.	sick	7.	his
2.	sleep	8.	week
3.	sit	9.	feel
4.	see	10.	sink
5.	street	11.	knee
6.	drink	12.	listen

Page 133, Exercise B

1.	sick	6.	week
2.	in	7.	listen
3.	knee	8.	practice
4.	it	9.	feel
5.	teeth	10.	sleeves

UNIT 12

Page 144, Exercises A and C

My name is Monika. I have my first job interview in the United States on Thursday. I feel confident. I practiced my interview skills in my English class. I need to remember three important things. I need to get to the interview early. I need to remember to shake hands firmly. I need to make eye contact. Wish me luck!

Page 145, Exercise B

1. doctor
2. bus
3. custodian
4. dollar
5. hospital
6. drugstore

Page 145, Exercise C

1. doctor
2. bus
3. shop
4. job
5. stop
6. up
7. custodian
8. number
9. problem
10. customer

Answer Key

UNIT 1

Page 2, Exercise A

1. Canada
2. the United States
3. Mexico
4. Haiti
5. El Salvador
6. Peru
7. Russia
8. Korea
9. China
10. Somalia
11. Cambodia
12. Vietnam

Page 3, Exercise B

1. A: What's your name?
   B: My name is _Maria_.
   A: Where are you from?
   B: I'm from _El Salvador_.
2. A: What's your name?
   B: My name is _Rosa_.
   A: Where are you from?
   B: I'm from _Haiti_.
3. A: What's your name?
   B: My name is _Teng_.
   A: Where are you from?
   B: I'm from _China_.

Page 3, Exercise C

Answers will vary.

Page 4, Exercise A

A B _C_ D E _F_ G _H_ I _J_ K L M N O
_P_ _Q_ R _S_ T U _V_ W _X_ _Y_ Z

Page 4, Exercise B

a _b_ c _d_ e f g h _i_ j k _l_ m _n_ o p q _r_
s _t_ u v _w_ x y _z_

Page 4, Exercise C

1. First name: Hong
   Last name: Chen
2. First name: Anna
   Last name: Novak
3. First name: Mark
   Last name: Smith
4. First name: Carla
   Last name: Diaz

Page 5, Exercise A

1. 3
2. 1
3. 8
4. 6
5. 4
6. 9
7. 5
8. 0
9. 7
10. 2

Page 5, Exercise B

1. 53691
2. 02469
3. 26750
4. 63980

Page 5, Exercise C

1. _67_4-555-_5 8 3 1_
2. _82_9-555-_1 1 9 4_
3. _42_7-555-_6 8 5 0_
4. _3 5 0_-555-_7 4 4 8_
5. _9 1 4_-555-_8 1 3 2_
6. _2 0_1-555-_4 9 9 0_

Page 6, Exercise A

1. am
2. are
3. are
4. am
5. are
6. am
7. are
8. am

Page 6, Exercise B

1. You
2. I
3. I
4. You
5. I
6. You
7. You
8. I

Page 6, Exercise C

1. You're Vue Moua.
2. I'm from Haiti.
3. I'm a new student.
4. You're the teacher.
5. I'm from the United States.
6. You're a student.
7. You're in the library.
8. I'm your classmate.

Page 7, Exercise A

1. She
2. He
3. He
4. She

Page 7, Exercise B

1. b   2. c   3. d   4. a

Page 8, Exercise C

1. a
2. b
3. a
4. a
5. b
6. a
7. b
8. b

Page 8, Exercise D

1. Mary is my classmate.
   She is my classmate.
   She's my classmate.
2. Mr. Smith is from Canada.
   He is from Canada.
   He's from Canada.
3. Ho-Jin is my friend.
   He is my friend.
   He's my friend.
4. Ms. Rivera is a good teacher.
   She is a good teacher.
   She's a good teacher.
5. Barbara is from Poland.
   She is from Poland.
   She's from Poland.

Page 9, Exercise A

1. is
2. are
3. is
4. are
5. are
6. is
7. is
8. are

Page 10, Exercise B

1. a   3. a   5. b
2. b   4. c   6. c

Page 10, Exercise C

1. They're from Vietnam.
2. We're new students.
3. You're my friends.
4. They're classmates.
5. You're good teachers.
6. We're from Poland.
7. They're friends.
8. You're good students.
9. We're friends.
10. They're from Russia.
11. We're in the library.
12. You're classmates.

Page 11, Exercise B

Page 12, Exercise A

_6_ Other students say hello and kiss.

_7_ How do you say hello?

_1_ My name is Ivan. I'm a student.

_4_ Some students say hello and hug.

_2_ I say hello to a classmate and
I smile.

_5_ Some students say hello and bow.

_3_ In my school, some students say
hello and shake hands.

Page 12, Exercise B

1. My name is Ivan. I'm a student.
2. I say hello to a classmate and
I smile.
3. In my school, some students say
hello and shake hands.
4. Some students say hello and hug.
5. Some students say hello and bow.
6. Other students say hello and kiss.
7. How do you say hello?

Page 13, Exercise A

1. map
2. phone
3. my
4. China
5. Mexico
6. number
7. classroom
8. students
9. nice
10. from
11. listen
12. meet

Page 13, Exercise B

1. map
2. answer
3. number
4. my
5. welcome
6. friend
7. students
8. listen
9. nice
10. phone

UNIT 2

Page 14, Exercise A

1. b	4. c	7. i
2. e	5. h	8. f
3. d	6. a	9. g

Page 15, Exercise B

1. b	3. a	5. b
2. b	4. a	

Page 15, Exercise C

1. Yes, I do.
2. No, I don't.
3. No, I don't.
4. Yes, I do.
5. Yes, I do.

Page 16, Exercise A

1. Turn on
2. Close
3. Turn off
4. Put away
5. Take out
6. Open

Page 17, Exercise C

1. Yes	3. Yes	5. Yes
2. No	4. No	

Page 17, Exercise D

1. Don't close your book.
2. Don't use a pencil.
3. Don't turn on the light.
4. Don't take out your notebook.
5. Don't open the door.
6. Don't put away your dictionary.

Page 18, Exercise A

1. classroom
2. women's room
3. computer lab
4. office
5. bookstore
6. testing room
7. library
8. men's room
9. cafeteria

Page 19, Exercise B

1. a	3. a	5. a
2. b	4. a	6. b

Page 20, Exercise A

1. next to
2. across from
3. across from
4. across from
5. next to
6. next to

Page 20, Exercise B

Answers will vary.

Page 21, Exercise B

1. Yes	4. No
2. No	5. Yes
3. No	6. Yes

Page 21, Exercise C

Answers will vary.

Page 22, Exercise A

1. c	3. e	5. f
2. d	4. b	6. a

Page 23, Exercise B

A: How do you study English?

B: I _go_ to class, and I _ask_ the teacher
questions.

A: That's great!

B: How do you study English?

A: I _practice_ with my classmates. At
home, I _write_ in my notebook.

Page 23, Exercise C

1. use
2. read
3. study
4. talk
5. write
6. ask
7. go
8. write
9. practice
10. go

Page 23, Exercise D

Answers will vary

Page 24, Exercise A

<u>2</u> In my country, students don't talk in class.
<u>4</u> In the United States, students talk in groups.
<u>6</u> My teacher listens to the students.
<u>1</u> My name is Lan.
<u>3</u> They listen to the teacher.
<u>5</u> In my class, students ask many questions.

Page 24, Exercise B

1. My name is Lan.
2. In my country, students don't talk in class.
3. They listen to the teacher.
4. In the United States, students talk in groups.
5. In my class, students ask many questions.
6. My teacher listens to the students.

Page 25, Exercise A

1. pen
2. notebook
3. pencil
4. book
5. piece of paper
6. backpack

Page 25, Exercise C

1. pen
2. practice
3. library
4. paper
5. number
6. open
7. birth
8. backpack
9. book
10. notebook

UNIT 3

Page 26, Exercise A

1. b   3. a   5. b
2. b   4. a   6. a

Page 26, Exercise B

1. b   3. c   5. a
2. e   4. f   6. d

Page 27, Exercise C

1. 8:10
2. 3:05
3. 7:15
4. 5:20
5. 12:30
6. 9:45

Page 28, Exercise A

1. A: <u>What</u> time is your English class?
   B: It's <u>from</u> 1:00 to 5:00.
   A: What <u>time</u> is your break?
   B: It's <u>at</u> 2:15.
2. A: What <u>time</u> is your English class?
   B: It's from 6:00 <u>to</u> 9:00.
   A: What time <u>is</u> your break?
   B: It's <u>at</u> 7:45.

Page 28, Exercise B

1. a   2. b   3. b   4. a

Page 28, Exercise C

1. It's from <u>9:15</u> to <u>1:15</u>.
2. It's from <u>11:15</u> to <u>11:45</u>.
3. It's from <u>12:30</u> to <u>4</u> OR <u>4:00</u>.
4. It's from <u>2</u> OR <u>2:00</u> to <u>2:20</u>.

Page 29, Exercise D

1. Yes   4. No
2. No   5. Yes
3. No   6. Yes

Page 29, Exercise E

1. The library is open at 9:00.
2. My break is from 2:00 to 2:20.
3. The cafeteria is open from 7:00 to 3:00.
4. My computer class starts at 4:30.
5. The office is open at 11:30.
6. My English class is from 10:00 to 12:00.
7. The computer lab is open from 8:00 to 11:00.
8. My break is over at 3:00.

Page 30, Exercise A

1. c   4. f   7. d
2. e   5. a   8. b
3. h   6. i   9. g

Page 31, Exercise B

Answers will vary.

Page 31, Exercise C

1. goes
2. takes
3. gets
4. eats
5. gets up
6. goes

Page 31, Exercise D

1. a   3. b   5. b
2. b   4. a

Page 32, Exercise A

Sunday	Monday	Tuesday	Wednesday	Thursday	Friday	Saturday
	Work 8–4	Class 11–3	Work 8–4	Class 11–3	Work 8–4	Work 10–2

Page 32, Exercise B

1. a   3. b   5. b
2. b   4. a

Page 32, Exercise C

1. from / to
2. on
3. on
4. from / to
5. on
6. from / to

Page 33, Exercise E

1. Yes   5. No
2. Yes   6. Yes
3. No   7. No
4. No   8. Yes

Page 34, Exercise A

1. b   6. f
2. h   7. j
3. a   8. e
4. g   9. d
5. i   10. c

Page 34, Exercise B

1. 25   7. 74
2. 37   8. 49
3. 62   9. 51
4. 70   10. 84
5. 98   11. 43
6. 100   12. 96

Page 34, Exercise C

1. two
2. ten
3. three
4. twenty

Page 35, Exercise D

1. seventy-one
2. fifty-nine
3. eleven
4. sixty
5. thirty-three
6. fourteen
7. one hundred
8. ninety
9. forty-seven
10. eighty-six

Page 35, Exercise E

1. b   2. a   3. b   4. c

Page 35, Exercise F

1. 93   5. 20
2. 80   6. 79
3. 17   7. 100
4. 13   8. 44

Page 36, Exercise A

_3_ He gets to work at 6:50. He starts work at 7:00.
_5_ He is always early for class.
_1_ Carlo likes to be on time.
_6_ On weekends, Carlo meets friends. He is always late!
_2_ He gets up early and gets ready for work.
_4_ Carlo goes to school after work.

Page 36, Exercise B

1. Carlo likes to be on time.
2. He gets up early and gets ready for work.
3. He gets to work at 6:50. He starts work at 7:00.
4. Carlo goes to school after work.
5. He is always early for class.
6. On weekends, Carlo meets friends. He is always late!

Page 37, Exercise A

1. dinner
2. twenty
3. time
4. don't
5. fifteen
6. two
7. Thursday
8. Sunday
9. Monday
10. get dressed
11. eat breakfast
12. twenty-two

Page 37, Exercise B

1. dinner
2. time
3. do
4. twelve
5. ten
6. does
7. get
8. read
9. day
10. breakfast

UNIT 4

Page 38, Exercise A

1. a   4. a   7. a
2. a   5. b   8. b
3. b   6. b   9. a

Page 39, Exercise B

1. father
2. wife
3. husband
4. brother
5. mother
6. daughter
7. grandfather
8. sister
9. grandmother
10. son

Page 40, Exercise B

1. a   3. b   5. a   7. b
2. b   4. a   6. b   8. a

Page 40, Exercise C

Answers will vary.

Page 41, Exercise D

Singular	Plural
parent	parents
brother	brothers
child	children
sister	sisters
daughter	daughters
son	sons
grandparent	grandparents

Page 41, Exercise E

1. sisters
2. parents
3. grandparents
4. brothers
5. children

Page 42, Exercise A

1. vacuum
2. make dinner
3. wash the dishes
4. take out the garbage
5. do the laundry
6. clean the house

Page 43, Exercise B

1. A: Who vacuums?
   B: vacuums
2. A: Who makes dinner?
   B: makes dinner
3. A: Who takes out the garbage?
   B: takes out the garbage
4. A: Who cleans the house?
   B: cleans the house
5. A: Who does the laundry?
   B: does the laundry
6. A: Who washes the dishes
   B: washes the dishes

Page 43, Exercise C

Answers will vary.

Page 44, Exercise A

1. January
2. February
3. March
4. April
5. May
6. June
7. July
8. August
9. September
10. October
11. November
12. December

Page 44, Exercise B

1. b   3. a   5. a
2. a   4. b   6. b

Page 45, Exercise A

Number	Month
1	January
2	February
3	March
4	April
5	May
6	June
7	July
8	August
9	September
10	October
11	November
12	December

Page 45, Exercise B

1. i   4. b   7. j   9. g
2. d   5. c   8. f   10. e
3. a   6. h

Page 46, Exercise C

1. April 14, 1998   4/14/98
2. June 17, 1985   6/17/85
3. September 1, 2007   9/1/07
4. February 22, 1974   2/22/74
5. March 21, 2010   3/21/10
6. November 29, 1999   11/29/99
7. July 13, 2002   7/13/02
8. January 8, 1995   1/8/95
9. October 19, 1968   10/19/68
10. May 31, 1983   5/31/83

Page 46, Exercise D

1. ⑥/20/93
2. 9/㉚/04
3. 12/6/⑦2
4. ⑤/30/06
5. 10/⑰/58
6. 1/9/⑧
7. ②/25/80
8. 11/④/97
9. 4/2/⑬

Page 47, Exercise B

Adult Education Center

Name: Pawel (First) Michal (Middle) Jasinski (Last)

Date of Birth: 6/1/86   Place of Birth: Poland

Class: ESL-2   Teacher: Mrs. Johnson

Class Schedule: Tuesday and Thursday (Day/s)   2:00–5:00 P.M. (Time)   12 (Room)

Page 48, Exercise A

2 In their country, men go to work.
5 Ernesto helps at home. He does the dishes.
1 Ernesto and Maria are married.
6 Sometimes Ernesto goes to the supermarket, too.
3 In their country, women stay at home. They do all the household chores.
4 In the United States, both Maria and Ernesto go to work.

Page 48, Exercise B

1. Ernesto and Maria are married.
2. In their country, men go to work.
3. In their country, women stay at home. They do all the household chores.
4. In the United States, both Maria and Ernesto go to work.
5. Ernesto helps at home. He does the dishes.
6. Sometimes Ernesto goes to the supermarket, too.

Page 49, Exercise A

1. dishes
2. third
3. date
4. mother
5. husband
6. daughter
7. there
8. laundry
9. brother
10. grandfather
11. thirteenth
12. grandmother

Page 49, Exercise B

1. dishes
2. the
3. they
4. laundry
5. that
6. month
7. father
8. December
9. date
10. there

UNIT 5

Page 50, Exercise A

1. b   3. a   5. e
2. d   4. f   6. c

Page 50, Exercise B

1. a quarter
2. a nickel
3. a half-dollar
4. a dime
5. a dollar coin

Page 51, Exercise C

1. B: Yes, I have a _quarter_, six _dimes_, and three _nickels_.
2. B: Yes. I have two _dimes_ and a _nickel_.
3. B: Yes. I have three _quarters_, two _dimes_, and a _nickel_.
4. B: Yes. I have four _nickels_ and five _pennies_.
5. B: Yes. I have two _quarters_ and five _dimes_.

Page 52, Exercise A

1. ten
2. twenty
3. five
4. one hundred
5. fifty
6. one

Page 53, Exercise B

1. twenty dollars
2. ten dollars
3. fifty dollars
4. one hundred dollars

Page 53, Exercise C

1. A: five
   B: singles
2. A: fifty
   B: tens
3. A: ten
   B: five
4. A: hundred
   B: twenty

Page 54, Exercise A

1. toothpaste
2. paper towels
3. shaving cream
4. toilet paper
5. soap
6. batteries
7. razor blades
8. deodorant
9. tissues
10. shampoo
11. lightbulbs
12. aspirin

Page 55, Exercise B

1. is   5. are
2. are   6. are
3. is   7. is
4. is   8. is

Page 55, Exercise C

1. Where is
2. Where are
3. Where are
4. Where is
5. Where is

Page 56, Exercise A

1. a   3. b   5. a
2. b   4. a

Page 57, Exercise B

1. 22¢   4. 16¢
2. 78¢   5. 43¢
3. 64¢   6. 97¢

Page 57, Exercise C

1. $1.59
2. $86.49
3. $7.28
4. $59.63
5. $95.40
6. $32.15

Page 57, Exercise D

1. $1.75
2. $4.78
3. $6.29
4. $1.60
5. $3.15
6. $2.20

Page 58, Exercise B

1. Yes   4. No
2. No   5. Yes
3. No

Page 58, Exercise C

1. $1.79
2. $2.79
3. $5.19
4. $1.44
5. $19.00

Page 59, Exercise D

Page 60, Exercise A

_3_ I get good bargains.
_1_ My name is Edna. In my country, I shop at markets.
_6_ How do I get good bargains? I buy things on sale!
_5_ I pay the price on the price tag.
_2_ I talk to the salespeople about the prices.
_4_ In the United States, I shop in big stores.

Page 60, Exercise B

1. My name is Edna. In my country, I shop at markets.
2. I talk to the salespeople about the prices.
3. I get good bargains.
4. In the United States, I shop in big stores.
5. I pay the price on the price tag.
6. How do I get good bargains? I buy things on sale!

Page 61, Exercise A

1. go
2. shaving cream
3. big
4. country
5. get
6. computer
7. price tag
8. count
9. good
10. drugstore
11. cash
12. coin

Page 61, Exercise B

1. go
2. cash
3. computer
4. good
5. count
6. big
7. price tag
8. drugstore
9. coin
10. get

UNIT 6

Page 62, Exercise A

1. tomatoes
2. onions
3. cucumbers
4. mushrooms
5. peas
6. carrots
7. lettuce
8. peppers
9. potatoes

Page 63, Exercise B

1. a	3. b	5. b
2. a	4. a	6. b

Page 63, Exercise D

1. b	3. b	5. b
2. b	4. a	6. a

Page 64, Exercise A

1. I <u>like potatoes</u>.
   I <u>don't like peppers</u>.
2. We <u>like tomatoes</u>.
   We <u>don't like onions</u>.
3. They <u>like peas</u>.
   They <u>don't like lettuce</u>.
4. Bernard and Sue <u>like cucumbers</u>.
   They <u>don't like carrots</u>.

Page 65, Exercise B

1. B: I like <u>peas</u>.
   I don't like <u>onions</u>.
2. B: I like <u>potatoes</u>.
   I don't like <u>peppers</u>.
3. B: I like <u>tomatoes</u>.
   I don't like <u>mushrooms</u>.
4. B: I like <u>cucumbers</u>.
   I don't like <u>carrots</u>.

Page 65, Exercise C

Answers will vary.

Page 66, Exercise A

1. apples
2. cherries
3. mangoes
4. strawberries
5. pears
6. oranges
7. bananas
8. peaches
9. grapes

Page 67, Exercise B

1. likes
2. likes
3. doesn't like
4. likes
5. doesn't like
6. doesn't like

Page 67, Exercise C

1. likes grapes
2. doesn't like strawberries
3. likes bananas
4. doesn't like apples
5. likes mangoes
6. doesn't like peaches

Page 68, Exercise A

1. a can of soup
2. a bag of rice
3. a loaf of bread
4. a gallon of milk
5. a box of cereal
6. a dozen eggs

Page 69, Exercise B

1. B: We need two (gallon) <u>gallons</u> of milk and two (box) <u>boxes</u> of cereal.
2. B: We need four (pound) <u>pounds</u> of chicken and three (bag) <u>bags</u> of rice.
3. B: We need two (loaf) <u>loaves</u> of bread and three (box) <u>boxes</u> of cereal.
4. B: We need three (pound) <u>pounds</u> of fish and five (can) <u>cans</u> of soup.

Page 69, Exercise C

1. B: Yes. I need a <u>loaf of bread</u> and two <u>gallons of milk</u>.
2. B: Yes. I need a <u>box of cereal</u> and two <u>bags of rice</u>.
3. B: Yes. I need two <u>dozen eggs</u> and three <u>cans of soup</u>.
4. B: Yes. I need a <u>gallon of milk</u> and two <u>boxes of cereal</u>.

Page 70, Exercise B

1. $1.59
2. $4.99
3. $1.78
4. $3.59
5. $2.18

Page 70, Exercise C

1 gallon of milk

3 cans of soup

2 boxes of cereal

2 lbs. of fish

2 dozen eggs

Page 71, Exercise A

1. d   3. a   5. e
2. c   4. b   6. f

Page 71, Exercise B

1. a   3. b   5. a
2. b   4. b

Page 72, Exercise A

_2_ Sometimes children eat with their fingers.

_6_ How do you eat in your country?

_3_ My name is Kyoko. In my country, people usually drink their soup.

_1_ My name is Tran. In my country, people usually eat with chopsticks.

_4_ In the United States, people usually eat with forks, knives, and spoons.

_5_ Sometimes they eat food with their fingers, like sandwiches and French fries.

Page 72, Exercise B

1. My name is Tran. In my country, people usually eat with chopsticks.
2. Sometimes children eat with their fingers.
3. My name is Kyoko. In my country, people usually drink their soup.
4. In the United States, people usually eat with forks, knives, and spoons.
5. Sometimes they eat food with their fingers, like sandwiches and French fries.
6. How do you eat in your country?

Page 73, Exercise A

1. fruit
2. vegetables
3. very
4. food
5. fish
6. have
7. beef
8. coffee
9. live
10. fifteen
11. five
12. favorite

Page 73, Exercise B

1. fruit
2. vegetables
3. Friday
4. food
5. live
6. fish
7. have
8. five
9. favorite
10. beef

UNIT 7

Page 74, Exercise A

1. bedroom
2. bathroom
3. closet
4. living room
5. dining room
6. kitchen
7. laundry room
8. basement
9. garage

Page 75, Exercise B

A: Guess what? I have a new apartment.
B: Really? What's it like?
A: It has two _bedrooms_, two _bathrooms_, a _kitchen_, and a _living room_.
B: It sounds great!

Page 75, Exercise D

1. Yes   4. No
2. No   5. Yes
3. Yes   6. No

Page 76, Exercise A

1. c   2. a   3. d   4. b

Page 76, Exercise B

1. B: There is a _sunny_ living room and a _small_ kitchen.
2. B: There is a _large_ garage and a _sunny_ dining room.
3. B: There is a _large_ closet and a _small_ basement.
4. B: There is a _sunny_ bedroom and a _modern_ kitchen.
5. B: There is a _large_ kitchen and a _modern_ bathroom.

Page 77, Exercise C

1. is   6. are
2. are   7. is
3. are   8. is
4. is   9. are
5. is   10. is

Page 77, Exercise D

1. There is
2. There are
3. There is
4. There is
5. There are
6. There is
7. There are
8. There is
9. There is
10. There are

Page 78, Exercise A

1. washing machine
2. dishwasher
3. dresser
4. stove
5. bed
6. sofa
7. refrigerator
8. dryer
9. lamp
10. chair
11. table
12. sink

Page 79, Exercise B

1. A: Is there
   B: there is
2. A: Are there
   B: there aren't
3. A: Are there
   B: there aren't
4. A: Is there
   B: there isn't
5. A: Are there
   B: there are
6. A: Is there
   B: there is

Page 79, Exercise C

1. a   3. a   5. b
2. b   4. b   6. a

Page 80, Exercise A

1. _14_ Cherry Lane
2. 1498 _Bank_ Street
3. 5 City _Boulevard_
4. 910 _River Road_
5. _34 Park_ Avenue
6. 527 Lake _Drive_
7. _14_ Cherry _Lane_
8. _1498 Bank Street_

Page 81, Exercise B

1. a   3. a   5. a
2. b   4. b   6. b

Page 81, Exercise C

1. 13   4. 20
2. 50   5. 184
3. 167   6. 1245

Page 82, Exercise A

1. d   3. e   5. c   7. b
2. g   4. f   6. a

Page 82, Exercise B

1. Yes   4. Yes
2. Yes   5. No
3. No

Page 83, Exercise C

1. Yes   4. Yes
2. Yes   5. No
3. No

Page 83, Exercise D

Answers will vary.

Page 84, Exercise A

_4_ Alicia has a good job.
_6_ But Alicia's parents are not happy.
_1_ Alicia is 21 years old.
_9_ What should Alicia do?
_2_ She is single.
_7_ In their country, single people live with their families.
_5_ Now she wants to move to an apartment with her friends.
_8_ In the United States, single people often live alone or with friends.
_3_ Alicia lives with her older sister and her brother-in-law in California.

Page 84, Exercise B

Alicia is 21 years old. She is single. Alicia lives with her older sister and her brother-in-law in California. Alicia has a good job. Now she wants to move to an apartment with her friends. But Alicia's parents are not happy. In their country, single people live with their families. In the United States, single people often live alone or with friends. What should Alicia do?

Page 85, Exercise A

1. dishwasher
2. dresser
3. table
4. chair
5. refrigerator
6. lamp

Page 85, Exercise C

1. dishwasher
2. large
3. room
4. lamp
5. address
6. closet
7. boulevard
8. road
9. living room
10. refrigerator

UNIT 8

Page 86, Exercise A

1. sneakers
2. pants
3. a shirt
4. shoes
5. a blouse
6. a skirt
7. a jacket
8. a dress
9. jeans
10. a sweater
11. socks
12. a T-shirt

Page 87, Exercise B

1. b   3. b   5. a
2. a   4. c   6. a

Page 87, Exercise C

1. A: jacket
   B: shoes
2. A: pants
   B: blouse
3. A: sweater
   B: shirt
4. A: sneakers
   B: jeans

Page 88, Exercise A

1. A: Can I help you?
   B: Do you have this shirt in a <u>large</u>?
   A: Yes. Here you go.
   B: Do you have these sneakers in a size <u>11</u>?
   A: I'm sorry. We don't.
2. A: Can I help you?
   B: Do you have this blouse in a <u>medium</u>?
   A: Yes. Here you go.
   B: Do you have these jeans in a size <u>10</u>?
   A: I'm sorry. We don't.
3. A: Can I help you?
   B: Do you have this T-shirt in an <u>extra large</u>?
   A: Yes. Here you go.
   B: Do you have these shoes in a size <u>12</u>?
   A: I'm sorry. We don't.

Page 88, Exercise B

1. this
2. this
3. These
4. This
5. these

Page 89, Exercise C

1. that
2. those
3. That
4. Those
5. that
6. those

Page 89, Exercise D

1. those
2. this
3. these
4. that

Page 90, Exercise A

1. red
2. green
3. orange
4. brown
5. yellow
6. blue
7. white
8. black
9. purple
10. gray
11. pink
12. beige

Page 90, Exercise B

1. yellow
2. orange
3. orange
4. green
5. red
6. green
7. red
8. green
9. red
10. orange OR yellow

Page 90, Exercise C

1. a
2. a
3. b
4. a
5. a
6. b
7. b
8. a

Page 91, Exercise E

1. Yes
2. No
3. No
4. Yes
5. No
6. Yes

Page 91, Exercise F

Answers will vary.

Page 91, Exercise G

Answers will vary.

Page 92, Exercise A

1. small
2. short
3. long
4. big

Page 92, Exercise B

1. The jacket is too small.
2. The sneakers are too big.
3. The dress is too long.
4. The pants are too short.

Page 93, Exercise C

1. A: I need to return a <u>sweater</u> and some <u>socks</u>.
   B: What's the problem?
   A: The <u>sweater</u> is too <u>long</u> OR <u>big</u> and the <u>socks</u> are too <u>big</u>. Here's my receipt.
2. A: I need to return a <u>dress</u> and some <u>pants</u>.
   B: What's the problem?
   A: The <u>dress</u> is too <u>long</u> and the <u>pants</u> are too <u>small</u>. Here's my receipt.

Page 93, Exercise D

1. b   2. b   3. b   4. a

Page 94, Exercise B

1. Yes
2. No
3. No
4. No
5. Yes
6. Yes

Page 95, Exercise C

1. Clara's
2. Thursday
3. 9:00
4. $15.50
5. $25.00
6. $19.99

Page 96, Exercise A

<u>4</u> In my country, people wear white for funerals.
<u>1</u> My name is Yun.
<u>3</u> I want to wear a long white dress.
<u>7</u> What should I do?
<u>2</u> My wedding is in August.
<u>5</u> Women wear a red and green dress on their wedding day.
<u>6</u> My mother and grandmother want me to wear a red and green dress.

Page 96, Exercise B

My name is Yun. My wedding is in August. I want to wear a long white dress. In my country, people wear white for funerals. Women wear a red and green dress on their wedding day. My mother and grandmother want me to wear a red and green dress. What should I do?

Page 97, Exercise A

1. skirt
2. shirt
3. shoes
4. sweater
5. pants
6. T-shirt

Page 97, Exercise C

1. skirt
2. she
3. small
4. shopping
5. T-shirt
6. short
7. size
8. sale
9. suit
10. should

UNIT 9

Page 98, Exercise A

1. c   4. e   7. a
2. f   5. g   8. d
3. i   6. b   9. h

Page 99, Exercise B

1. Yes   4. Yes
2. Yes   5. No
3. No   6. No

Page 99, Exercise C

Answers will vary.

Page 100, Exercise A

1. playing the guitar
2. going to the library
3. reading the newspaper
4. going to the movies

Page 101, Exercise B

1. She's using e-mail.
2. You're reading the newspaper.
3. They're watching TV.
4. We're listening to music.
5. He's going to the movies.
6. I'm playing soccer.
7. She's exercising.
8. You're visiting friends.
9. I'm playing the guitar.

Page 101, Exercise C

1. He's playing soccer.
2. We're going to the movies.
3. I'm reading the newspaper.
4. He's exercising.
5. They're using e-mail.
6. You're watching TV.
7. She's playing the guitar.
8. I'm visiting friends.
9. She's listening to music.

Page 102, Exercise A

1. talk on the phone
2. do homework
3. make dinner
4. take out the garbage
5. pay bills
6. do the laundry
7. wash the car
8. walk the dog
9. clean the house

Page 103, Exercise B

1. he is
2. he isn't OR he's not
3. she is
4. I'm not
5. they are
6. they aren't OR they're not

Page 103, Exercise C

1. Are you washing the car?
2. Is Darya paying the bills?
3. Are Ivan and Sara studying English?
4. Are they cleaning the house?
5. Is he taking out the garbage?
6. Is Ya-Wen playing soccer?

Page 103, Exercise D

Answers will vary.

Page 104, Exercise A

1. fix cars
2. answer the phone
3. work on the computer
4. look for something
5. help a customer
6. take orders
7. take a break
8. count money
9. drive a truck

Page 105, Exercise B

1. he's not
2. they're not
3. I'm not
4. she's not
5. he's not

Page 105, Exercise C

1. She's not driving a truck.
2. He's not answering the phone.
3. They're not counting money.
4. He's not working on the computer.

Page 106, Exercise A

MESSAGE

For: Mr. Brown   Date: March 14

Caller: Carlos Rivera   Phone: 718-555-3746

Message: He's not coming to school today.

Page 106, Exercise B

MESSAGE

For: Mrs. Smith   Date: September 4

Caller: Jane Reynolds   Phone: 857-555-3854

Message: She's not coming to work today.

Page 107, Exercise C

1.
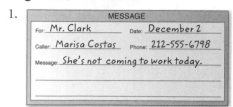

MESSAGE	
For: Mr. Clark	Date: December 2
Caller: Marisa Costas	Phone: 212-555-6798
Message: She's not coming to work today.	

2.

MESSAGE	
For: Kyoko	Date: March 19
Caller: Ann	Phone: 512-555-9841
Message: She's not going to the movies today.	

3.

MESSAGE	
For: Ms. Popova	Date: February 8
Caller: Sam White	Phone: 479-555-8310
Message: He's not coming to class today.	

Page 108, Exercise A

_4_ They talk on the phone and go shopping.

_9_ Then they spend time relaxing and talking.

_10_ What do you do on weekends?

_6_ On weekends, my wife and I eat alone.

_5_ They play sports and watch TV.

_1_ My name is Alfonso.

_7_ Our children don't sit down with us to eat.

_2_ I have two children.

_3_ They are busy every weekend with their friends.

_11_ Do you spend time with your family or friends?

_8_ In my country, families eat together on weekends.

Page 108, Exercise B

My name is Alfonso. I have two children. They are busy every weekend with their friends. They talk on the phone and go shopping. They play sports and watch TV. On weekends, my wife and I eat alone. Our children don't sit down with us to eat. In my country, families eat together on weekends. Then they spend time relaxing and talking. What do you do on weekends? Do you spend time with your family or friends?

Page 109, Exercise A

1. message
2. date
3. help
4. take
5. name
6. every
7. today
8. hello
9. exercise
10. newspaper
11. Wednesday
12. sentence

Page 109, Exercise B

1. message
2. yes
3. play
4. name
5. today
6. sentence
7. make
8. spend
9. later
10. help

UNIT 10

Page 110, Exercise A

1. c	4. b	7. i
2. e	5. a	8. d
3. g	6. h	9. f

Page 111, Exercise B

1. There's a parking lot on the corner of _North Street_ and _Fourth Avenue_.
2. There's a restaurant on the corner of _Main Street_ and _Fourth Avenue_.
3. There's a drugstore on the corner of _North Street_ and _Third Avenue_.
4. There's a hospital on the corner of _Main Street_ and _Second Avenue_.
5. There's a computer store on the corner of _Erie Street_ and _Second Avenue_.
6. There's a supermarket on the corner of _Main Street_ and _Third Avenue_.
7. There's a gas station on the corner of _Erie Street_ and _Third Avenue_.
8. There's a bank on the corner of _North Street_ and _Second Avenue_.
9. There's an ATM on the corner of _Erie Street_ and _Fourth Avenue_.

Page 112, Exercise A

1. post office
2. park
3. Department of Motor Vehicles (DMV)
4. City Hall
5. fire station
6. school
7. police station
8. library
9. court house

Page 113, Exercise B

1. across from
2. across from
3. between
4. across from
5. between
6. across from
7. across from
8. between

Page 114, Exercise A

1. g	4. h	7. b
2. c	5. a	8. d
3. e	6. i	9. f

Page 115, Exercise B

1. take the bus
2. take the train
3. take a taxi
4. drive

Page 115, Exercise C

Answers will vary.

Page 116, Exercise A

1. Turn left.
2. Turn right.
3. Go straight.

Page 116, Exercise B

1. B: It's on First Avenue. _Go straight_ for one block. Then _turn right_ on First Avenue.
2. B: It's on Second Avenue. _Turn left_ on Main Street. Then _go straight_ for one block.
3. B: It's on Third Avenue. _Turn right_ on Central Street. Then _turn left_ on Third Avenue.

Page 117, Exercise C

1. police station
2. library
3. bank
4. gas station

Page 118, Exercise A

1. walk/don't walk
2. no parking
3. stop sign
4. no U-turn
5. yield
6. one-way street
7. speed limit 25 miles per hour
8. train crossing
9. no left turn

Page 119, Exercise B

1. No	5. Yes
2. No	6. No
3. Yes	7. Yes
4. No	8. No

Page 120, Exercise A

_9_ I need to show the bank my business plan.
_5_ I have a dream.
_1_ My name is Hong.
_6_ I want to open my own restaurant here.
_7_ I need to go to City Hall for a business license.
_2_ In my country, I worked in a restaurant.
_4_ Here in the United States, I'm a cook, too.
_10_ Soon my family and friends can eat at my new restaurant!
_8_ I need to go to the bank for a loan.
_3_ I was a cook.

Page 120, Exercise B

My name is Hong. In my country, I worked in a restaurant. I was a cook. Here in the United States, I'm a cook, too. I have a dream. I want to open my own restaurant here. I need to go to City Hall for a business license. I need to go to the bank for a loan. I need to show the bank my business plan. Soon my family and friends can eat at my new restaurant!

Page 121, Exercise A

1. bike
2. library
3. taxi
4. bank
5. sign
6. gas station

Page 121, Exercise C

1. bike
2. answer
3. ride
4. gas
5. drive
6. thanks
7. family
8. license
9. write
10. sign

UNIT 11

Page 122, Exercise A

1. ear
2. eye
3. nose
4. neck
5. stomach
6. knee
7. foot
8. leg
9. hand
10. arm
11. chest
12. shoulder

Page 123, Exercise B

1. a	4. a	7. a
2. b	5. b	8. a
3. a	6. b	

Page 123, Exercise C

1. neck hurts
2. hand hurts
3. stomach hurts
4. shoulder hurts

Page 124, Exercise A

1. Breathe
2. sleeves
3. straight
4. Lie
5. jacket
6. mouth
7. out
8. Step
9. table

Page 125, Exercise B

a. 3   b. 1   c. 4   d. 2

Page 125, Exercise D

☑ 1. Joe gets a checkup every year.
☐ 2. Joe has a doctor's appointment on Tuesday.
☑ 3. His appointment is at the health clinic.
☐ 4. Joe gives the doctor instructions.
☑ 5. Joe is in good health.

Page 126, Exercise A

1. f   4. h   7. c
2. a   5. i   8. e
3. d   6. b   9. g

Page 127, Exercise B

1. take an aspirin
2. drink a lot of liquids
3. get a lot of rest
4. stay home from work

Page 127, Exercise C

1. You should take an aspirin.
2. You should stay home from school.
3. You should stay home from work.
4. You should drink a lot of liquids.

Page 128, Exercise A

1. Someone robbed my house.
2. There was a car accident.
3. My friend is having a heart attack.
4. There is a building on fire.

Page 128, Exercise B

1. a   2. a   3. b   4. b

Page 129, Exercise C

1. A: 911. What's your emergency?
    B: There is a building on _fire_.
    A: Where are you?
    B: _1402_ Oak Avenue in Park City.
    A: What's the cross street?
    B: Third Street.
2. A: 911. What's your emergency?
    B: My friend is having a _heart_ attack.
    A: Where are you?
    B: _8756_ Park Avenue in River City.
    A: What's the cross street?
    B: First Street.
3. A: 911. What's your emergency?
    B: Someone _robbed_ my house.
    A: Where are you?
    B: _4739_ Third Avenue in Maple City.
    A: What's the cross street?
    B: Main Street.
4. A: 911. What's your emergency?
    B: There was a _car_ accident.
    A: Where are you?
    B: _3289_ Fourth Avenue in Green City.
    A: What's the cross street?
    B: Lake Street.

Page 130, Exercise A

1. b   4. b   7. a
2. a   5. b   8. b
3. a   6. a   9. a

Page 130, Exercise B

1. Yes   4. Yes
2. No   5. No
3. Yes

Page 131, Exercise D

1. pain and fever
2. aspirin
3. 1 tablet
4. 6 hours
5. water
6. doctor

Page 132, Exercise A

_5_ My daughter is 23 years old.
_8_ But I feel healthy.
_1_ My name is Mariam.
_2_ I'm 45 years old.
_10_ Why should I go to a doctor?
_9_ I don't feel sick.
_4_ Now my family and I are in the United States.
_7_ She says it's important.
_6_ She says that women here have a checkup every year.
_3_ In my country, people go to the doctor when they are sick.

Page 132, Exercise B

My name is Mariam. I'm 45 years old. In my country, people go to the doctor when they are sick. Now my family and I are in the United States. My daughter is 23 years old. She says that women here have a checkup every year. She says it's important. But I feel healthy. I don't feel sick. Why should I go to a doctor?

Page 133, Exercise A

1. sick
2. sleep
3. sit
4. see
5. street
6. drink
7. his
8. week
9. feel
10. sink
11. knee
12. listen

Page 133, Exercise B

1. sick
2. in
3. knee
4. it
5. teeth
6. week
7. listen
8. practice
9. feel
10. sleeves

UNIT 12

Page 134, Exercise A

1. f   4. b   7. a
2. d   5. g   8. e
3. i   6. h   9. c

Page 135, Exercise B

1. A: a mechanic
   B: a homemaker
2. A: a construction worker
   B: a dentist
3. A: a bus driver
   B: a painter
4. A: a housekeeper
   B: a sales assistant

Page 136, Exercise A

1. a custodian
2. a security guard
3. a cashier
4. an office assistant
5. a factory worker
6. a doctor
7. a cook
8. a waiter
9. a nurse

Page 137, Exercise B

1. does   5. does
2. do   6. does
3. does   7. do
4. do   8. do

Page 137, Exercise C

1. Where do you work?
2. Where does Nancy work?
3. Where do they work?
4. Where does Rafal work?
5. Where do Tien and Monika work?
6. Where does she work?

Page 137, Exercise D

Answers will vary.

Page 138, Exercise A

1. fix cars
2. use a computer
3. speak two languages
4. build houses
5. help customers
6. drive a truck
7. use a cash register
8. help sick people
9. use office machines

Page 139, Exercise B

1. help customers
2. build houses
3. fix cars
4. help sick people
5. use a cash register
6. use office machines

Page 140, Exercise A

1. I can
2. he can't
3. she can't
4. they can
5. he can

Page 140, Exercise B

1. A: use a computer
   B: Answers will vary.
2. A: help customers
   B: Answers will vary.
3. A: help sick people
   B: Answers will vary.
4. A: build houses
   B: Answers will vary.

Page 141, Exercise C

1. A: Can Mrs. Smith speak two languages
   B: she can
2. A: Can Mr. Lim use a computer
   B: he can't
3. A: Can Ms. Popova fix cars
   B: she can
4. A: Can you build houses
   B: I can't
5. A: Can Eric and Katrina use a cash register
   B: they can
6. A: Can you help customers
   B: I can't
7. A: Can Mr. Nowak use office machines
   B: he can
8. A: Can Alex and Marie drive a truck
   B: they can't

Page 142, Exercise B

1. No   4. Yes
2. Yes   5. Yes
3. No

Page 143, Exercise D

1. A   3. A   5. A   7. B
2. B   4. A   6. B   8. A

Page 143, Exercise E

1. d   3. f   5. a
2. e   4. b   6. c

Page 143, Exercise F

Answers will vary.

Page 144, Exercise A

_6_ I need to get to the interview early.

_1_ My name is Monika.

_5_ I need to remember three important things.

_8_ I need to make eye contact.

_9_ Wish me luck!

_3_ I feel confident.

_7_ I need to remember to shake hands firmly.

_4_ I practiced my interview skills in my English class.

_2_ I have my first job interview in the United States on Thursday.

Page 144, Exercise B

My name is Monika. I have my first job interview in the United States on Thursday. I feel confident. I practiced my interview skills in my English class. I need to remember three important things. I need to get to the interview early. I need to remember to shake hands firmly. I need to make eye contact. Wish me luck!

Page 145, Exercise A

1. doctor
2. bus
3. custodian
4. dollar
5. hospital
6. drugstore

Page 145, Exercise C

1. doctor
2. bus
3. shop
4. job
5. stop
6. up
7. custodian
8. number
9. problem
10. customer

Audio CD Track List